Praise for *Not My Child*

*"If you have a teen who is caught up in the dark and destructive world of drug addiction, your entire family is at risk of facing pain and even disintegration. Dr. Lawlis's book **Not My Child** is nothing short of genius as it lights the path out of that perilous world. Frank and action oriented, it will become your go-to resource at this most critical time. A copy stays at my fingertips, and I have acquired this book in bulk to share with families in need."*

— **Dr. Phil McGraw**, host of the *Dr. Phil* show and
#1 *New York Times* best-selling author

"This is an essential book for all parents—those who feel that their child is immune to addictions, as well as those made numb from the stranglehold when their child becomes another statistic of an addiction. This book is particularly essential as it guides parents to effectively relate with their child in the throes of the addiction— after first helping parents examine themselves and confront their own fears, myths, and misconceptions. Dr. Frank Lawlis presents an invaluable, holistic framework to understand and treat these various catastrophic epidemics that claim and incapacitate the heart and soul of today's young people. Drawing on antidotes from an arsenal of medicine, neuroscience, healthy relationships, and the healing power of vital spirituality, he guides parents to reclaim an active, caring parenting role for their child to arrest the deadening destructiveness of addictions."

— **John T. Chirban, Ph.D., Th.D.**, Harvard Medical School

"As an intervention specialist, I work directly with families affected by addiction, and Dr. Lawlis's information from the latest neuroscience research will empower parents to stand up and say 'Not my child.' Dr. Lawlis gives readers a practical, compassionate, and insightful guide for families dealing with one of the biggest epidemics ravaging America: teen addiction. Based on years of clinical experience, Dr. Lawlis explains that addiction affects not just the addicted individual, but the entire family unit."

— **Debbie Knauss, RN, LCDC**, President/CEO,
VIP Recovery (www.viprecovery.com)

"Finally, a comprehensive look at the impact of addiction on the individual and the family! Dr. Lawlis draws on extensive experience, current neuroscience, and remarkable compassion to offer real and understandable solutions to dealing with addiction

in our most precious populations—teenagers and young adults. It is time that we stand up against our nation's most insidious epidemic. It will take a societal and cultural effort if we are to fight skillfully and successfully. Dr. Lawlis is a true leader in this fight, a man with courage, knowledge, and above all, <u>love</u> for those suffering from the disease of addictive illness. This is must-read for anyone who is ready to stand up and say, 'NOT MY CHILD'!"

— **Mandy Baker, M.S., LCDC,** Executive Clinical Director and Vice President, Origins Recovery Centers

NOT MY CHILD

ALSO BY DR. FRANK LAWLIS

The ADD Answer

The IQ Answer

Mending the Broken Bond

Retraining the Brain

The Brain Power Cookbook

The Autism Answer

The PTSD Breakthrough

Please visit:

Hay House USA: www.hayhouse.com®
Hay House Australia: www.hayhouse.com.au
Hay House UK: www.hayhouse.co.uk
Hay House South Africa: www.hayhouse.co.za
Hay House India: www.hayhouse.co.in

NOT MY CHILD

A PROGRESSIVE AND PROACTIVE APPROACH
for Healing Addicted Teenagers
and Their Families

DR. FRANK LAWLIS

HAY HOUSE, INC.
Carlsbad, California • New York City
London • Sydney • Johannesburg
Vancouver • Hong Kong • New Delhi

Published and distributed in the United States by: Hay House, Inc.: www.hayhouse.com® • *Published and distributed in Australia by:* Hay House Australia Pty. Ltd.: www.hayhouse.com.au • *Published and distributed in the United Kingdom by:* Hay House UK, Ltd.: www.hayhouse.co.uk • *Published and distributed in the Republic of South Africa by:* Hay House SA (Pty), Ltd.: www.hayhouse.co.za • *Distributed in Canada by:* Raincoast Books: www.raincoast.com • *Published in India by:* Hay House Publishers India: www.hayhouse.co.in

Cover design: Charles McStravick • *Interior design:* Tricia Breidenthal

Library of Congress Cataloging-in-Publication Data

Lawlis, G. Frank.
  Not my child : a progressive and proactive approach for healing addicted teenagers and their families / Dr. Frank Lawlis. -- 1st edition.
    pages cm
  Includes bibliographical references.
  ISBN 978-1-4019-4209-0 (hardcover : alk. paper) 1. Teenagers--Substance use. 2. Addicts--Rehabilitation. 3. Addicts--Family relationships. 4. Substance abuse--Treatment. I. Title.
  RJ506.D78L39 2013
  618.3'686--dc23
                                    2013029763

Hardcover ISBN: 978-1-4019-4209-0

16 15 14 13   6 5 4 3
1st edition, November 2013
3rd edition, November 2013

SUSTAINABLE FORESTRY INITIATIVE

Certified Chain of Custody
Promoting Sustainable Forestry

www.sfiprogram.org
SFI-01268

Printed in the United States of America

SFI label applies to the text stock

To the administration and staff of Origins Recovery Centers on South Padre Island, Texas, for their courage and their amazing skills. Their loving commitment to healing those under their care has been an inspiration to me— and their work serves as proof that there are healing angels on Earth.

CONTENTS

PART IV: HEALING RELATIONSHIPS AND SPIRITS

PREFACE

When I was a teenager, I lived in Levelland, a small town on the South Plains of the Texas Panhandle. My boyhood stomping grounds were dry—in terms of alcohol, that is. If adults wanted a beer or mixed drink, they had to drive 300 miles to Mexico to find the nearest bar. Levelland was in a dry county—but that didn't mean booze was not available.

Our preacher frequently railed about the "demons of drink" from his pulpit, and there were those who drank in abundance. I knew of some local tragedies related to drinking, but I didn't have much personal exposure to alcohol or drug addiction while growing up. Back then, people in my hometown didn't pop prescription pills to cure their ailments or to relieve their aches and pains. As far as I knew, the most prominent approach to pain was either to take a couple of aspirins or "bite the bullet" and hope it would go away.

My father had witnessed alcohol abuse while serving in the U.S. Army in World War II. As the owner and operator of the local airport, he had also witnessed several small plane crashes in which the pilots had been drinking. He warned me about the dangers of impaired judgment from drinking. I had a strong will; my mind was firmly set on playing professional football, so I took his advice and stayed sober—which is not to say my judgment was always that great, even with a clear mind!

My dreams of a pro football career did not work out, but I found a greater calling as a psychologist. I wanted to help young people and families overcome challenges in their lives to heal their relationships with each other. While I had little exposure to drug and alcohol addiction as a boy, my training and early experiences as a psychologist opened my eyes to the depth of the drug- and alcohol-abuse epidemic in American society. Later, I had to deal with this problem within my own family when my stepson became addicted to drugs. This book, then, is written from both professional and personal experience.

I am painfully aware that teenage drug and alcohol addiction affects not just the young person in the throes of addiction but the entire family, straining relationships and throwing lives into turmoil. Parents struggling with addicted teenagers have told me that their stricken children appear to have lost their souls, including their abilities to respond to and to give love. I've witnessed firsthand the anger and sense of betrayal generated in a family dealing with an addict. I've been attacked for trying to help. Sadly, I have been awakened many times at all hours of the night by drunken or drugged patients or acquaintances crying out for help.

I have a great empathy for families dealing with an addicted loved one. I also understand their frustrations and their anger over the insidious and unrelenting nature of addiction. I want you to understand up front that the challenges that must be overcome are considerable—but *there is hope*. Magical transformations can occur. I have seen many teenagers overcome addiction and return to joyful, productive, and loving lives.

I've written this book because the growing number of addicts and the limitations of current treatment programs for them have convinced me that we desperately need innovative strategies in the treatment and counseling programs for those addicted to drugs and alcohol—and for their families and loved ones, too. If long-standing approaches are not working—and they are not—then we need to find better and more effective ways to deal with addiction and its impact on society.

I want to share with you some powerful tools and techniques I've used to help families and individuals dealing with addiction. This book is intended as a manual for parents dealing with teenage drug and alcohol abuse. I offer you this material to help you understand your teenager and to assist you in assessing the level of addiction, as well as to give you a grasp of the available range of treatments that can help you regain the child you may feel you've lost. This book offers hope, scientific information, and spiritual encouragement.

As you read, know that your love for your child is a powerful ally. Every recovery plan should be built upon compassion and strong family bonds. My approach is unique in that it deals with the disease in a holistic, mind-body-spirit format based on new and revolutionary findings. I have spent more than 40 years developing and refining my methods. I began working in the field of addiction treatment in the 1960s, when I created a new diagnostic program for alcoholism. Later, I worked with the Texas Commission on Alcohol and Drug Abuse and helped write an educational grant for Texas Tech University. I consider alcohol and drug addiction a major threat around the world, and I am committed to developing innovative treatments.

I co-founded the Lawlis and Peavey PsychoNeuro-Plasticity Center (www.lawlispeavey.com) in Lewisville, Texas, where we practice innovative and holistic approaches for in-depth psychological assessments that take into account medical, psychological, neurological, sociological, and relationship considerations. We have had wonderful results with these methods. I don't claim that they work for every individual. Each case is different. The addicted brain can defy scientific understanding at times. Patience, love, and compassion are often the most critical aspects of treatment.

About This Book

This book is divided into four sections:

Part I defines the problem of teenage drug and alcohol addiction and its scope. The Introduction provides case studies that offer insight into the impact of teenage addiction on parents, siblings, other family members, and friends. It also looks at the depth of the problem in the United States and around the world, examines the challenges of finding treatments that work, and offers an overview of some new methods that show promise.

Chapter 1 looks at teenage addiction and drug and alcohol abuse from a societal viewpoint so you can put your teenager's challenges in context. The central message: you are not alone. Teenage addiction is an epidemic, and some of it is rooted in the widespread practice of overprescribing of medication.

Chapter 2 offers guidance in detecting and treating early signs of drug or alcohol abuse and addiction in teenagers. I note that just because a child manifests certain behaviors, such as hyperactivity or a short attention span, a parent shouldn't assume that the child is at risk—but these are indicators of a *potentially* at-risk child.

Part II of this book offers insights into the special aspects of the teenage brain that not only make the impact of drug and alcohol more destructive, but also provide for unique opportunities for treatment and recovery. Chapter 3 explains how drugs and alcohol impair judgment and encourage high-risk behavior in the still-developing teenage brain. Chapter 4 explains brain plasticity in teenagers, while Chapter 5 discusses opportunities for healing teenagers' brains.

Part III of the book offers tools for parents, family members, and others who want to be part of the solution to teenage addiction. Chapter 6 looks at methods for helping the addicted teenager deal with depression that, if left untreated, can lead to a deadly downward spiral. Chapter 7 offers guidance for treating the obsessive cravings that teenagers addicted to alcohol and drugs experience. Chapter 8 offers guidance in cases of teenage addiction and drug and alcohol abuse in which standard therapeutic approaches don't work. The alternative methods described offer a no-nonsense approach, with a strong spiritual emphasis.

Part IV offers guidance for healing family relationships with the addicted teenager, for proactive parenting, and for spiritual healing. Chapter 9 provides tools for enhancing mutual understanding, trust, respect, and communication among the addicted teenager and family members. Mending familial bonds can be a challenge. It requires patience, understanding, empathy, forgiveness, authenticity, and a well-constructed plan.

Chapter 10 offers my thoughts on the role of prayer in healing the teenage addict. I've seen prayer have powerful effects, although this is not intended to endorse any particular religious or spiritual beliefs. Consider this an optional approach, and feel free to adapt it to your beliefs.

Finally, in the Appendices, I offer a parenting parable, as well as information and resources you can call upon to increase your knowledge about teen addiction and get your child on the road to recovery.

You can either read this book from beginning to end or select chapters and sections that you find particularly relevant to your situation and circumstances. I do believe that reading the entire book will be of great benefit, of course, but I understand that parents of addicted teenagers are often hungry for specific guidance. My goal is to give you whatever you need to deal with your challenges . . . and to assure you that there is hope for better days ahead.

✦ ✦ ✦

Author's Note: Many of the stories in this book are true accounts in which the names and identifying details have been changed to protect confidentiality. Other stories, composites drawn from years of clinical work, are true to the spirit of teaching, although not to the experience of any particular person.

Disclaimer: I am all for trying innovative home remedies in many instances, but I also recommend psychotherapy and counseling. Such treatment can be enormously useful in helping to identify a teenager's personal triggers for drug and alcohol cravings.

PART I

UNDERSTANDING TEENAGE ADDICTION

Introduction

The Face of Teenage Addiction and the Threat to Your Family

Rest assured that I have seen many remarkable turn-arounds for addicted teenagers and their families. Bodies, minds, and spirits can be healed. Relationships can be restored.

One of my favorite examples of this is Antonio, a street-gang leader renowned for his ruthlessness and tenacity. He was the fifth of eight children raised by a mother whose love and faith were no match for Antonio's aggression. From a young age he established an almost mythic reputation for bloodletting, criminal behavior, and drug and alcohol abuse. The only "normal" part of his youth was his skill and dedication as an athlete. Antonio was gifted.

He was fast on his feet and possessed extraordinary endurance, but he was not so elusive that he escaped capture after robbing a 7-Eleven. At the age of 16, he was facing his first prison term. The judge had planned to sentence him to two years in a correctional institution, until Antonio's high-school cross-country coach stepped forward and volunteered to serve as his guardian and attempt to set him straight.

Antonio respected his coach, who understood his criminal tendencies and offered him a respite from drugs and alcohol through athletic competition. Antonio had a need to stand out from the crowd, and his coach convinced him that athletic achievement offered greater recognition, longer-term rewards, and a much more constructive outlet than burglary and assault.

Their shared goal was to win the state high-school cross-country championship and, in the process, help Antonio earn a college scholarship. Through strenuous workouts and unrelenting focus, they worked together. Over the course of two years, Antonio cleaned up his body and his mind. At the end of his senior year, he achieved his goals: a state cross-country trophy and a scholarship to a prestigious university, where he later earned both a bachelor's and a master's degree.

Antonio's story is more involved than I have portrayed it here in this limited space—but the point is that even some of the toughest addicts can turn their lives around in dramatic ways. No problem is completely intractable—but none is without challenges. Antonio's high school coach showed great faith and courage by stepping into his life. In some ways, it was easier for the coach to help than a parent because Antonio trusted him from the outset; the kind of deeply rooted hurts and lack of trust that often exist between an addict and his parents were not present in the relationship. Still, in my extensive experience, addicted teenagers can transform their lives and rebuild relationships if all sides are committed to forgiving, loving, and working together.

Believe me: where there is a will, there is a way—many ways, in fact.

Now let's look at a case that was much more complex, and less of a success story, but which offers valuable lessons.

Dorothy, a mother of three, was numb with worry as she walked up the driveway to her beautiful suburban home, where she'd lived for the past ten years. Even her beloved oak trees, with their strong, outstretched limbs, provided little comfort as she approached the front door. Her stomach was churning, and her mind raced with frightening scenarios of what she might encounter inside.

Her worst fears were realized when she saw that her 16-year-old daughter, Jennifer, had cleared out her bedroom, including her new flat-screen television. A quick search revealed that jewelry, keepsakes, and cash had been taken from their hiding places. Dorothy quietly wished that she were dealing with a burglar and a stranger rather than her daughter. Calling the police was not an option. Instead, she called Jenny, knowing that there was little hope of actually reaching the child she had once known and loved.

There was no answer, which was never a good sign.

Her troubled daughter finally called at midnight. Dorothy heard the resentment and anger in Jenny's tone.

"Jenny, did you take the television and my jewelry from the house?" she asked, already knowing the answer.

The response was belligerent and all too typical of their recent communications.

"Yes, why the hell not? F---, you told me to take whatever f---ing stuff I wanted, so I did. What? You want it back? Too late . . . it's gone. Are you gonna send me to jail? Ha ha! You f---ing bitch. Go ahead, I f---ing hate you anyway." With that, Jenny hung up the phone.

Dorothy tried to control her response, taking a deep breath as her mind searched for some helpful way to respond to her daughter's outrage. She called Jenny's cell again and was surprised when her daughter answered— but now, Dorothy's emotions overwhelmed her.

"Jenny, I never told you to steal from me!" Dorothy screamed into the phone. "And where the hell are you anyway?"

Her daughter responded with her own fury. "Whatever! I hate you, you lying bitch. You told me that if I wasn't happy, I could live somewhere else. Well, I'm not happy and I'm not your 'problem' anymore."

Then Dorothy heard a click and the phone call ended.

Dorothy sat in silence, trying to fathom how her bright, beautiful, and talented teenager could become a monster she no longer knew. Jenny had been given everything she wanted, and she had been a loving child until just a year ago. Now, Dorothy found herself unable to feel love for this demonic stranger. She no longer physically or emotionally resembled the beautiful honor student, cheerleader, and loving daughter she had been. Jenny was abusing her body as well as drugs. Her face and body bore sores and scars, the result of both a sexually transmitted disease and scratching. When Dorothy had asked her about these marks, Jenny would make no sense whatsoever in her explanations and instead would spew out venomous, hateful tirades that left Dorothy reeling as if she had been beaten.

✦ ✦

As her relationship with her daughter had deteriorated, Dorothy found that her mental and physical health was also declining. She could no longer keep down her food, which became less of a concern as her appetite dwindled. Her loss of weight and muscle tone mirrored her emotional meltdown.

Dorothy no longer considered herself a real mother, or a real person, and although she tried to focus all of her love on her son and other daughter, she was afraid of losing them to drugs, too. Her guilt and depression only heightened her fears and put stress on her other relationships. She felt she was failing on all fronts. Dorothy had become numb to everyone and everything around her because of this ordeal. She felt that she might never feel love again because of the damage done by her daughter's addiction.

She'd gotten her first glimmer of the problem just a few months earlier, when Jenny had been arrested with a group of teenagers for drinking. All of them were from affluent families. Initially, Dorothy was not overly concerned. She'd told herself that Jenny was just going through a stage and trying to fit in with the popular crowd. Dorothy remembered drinking while in high school, and she knew most of the other parents from this group had done the same thing. She brought her daughter home from the police station and gave her a stern warning, thinking that would be the end of it. Instead, Jenny's behavior rapidly deteriorated during the next eight months.

Her daughter was sent home twice for being drunk in school. On three other occasions, she was caught smoking marijuana. Dorothy called the parents of Jenny's friends in search of information. She discovered that her daughter was now hanging out with a different group. It was as if Jenny had become another person altogether. Her grades had dropped from A's and B's to D's and F's. Once a style queen, Jenny no longer seemed to care about her appearance. She'd become rebellious, and her mood swings were volatile and erratic.

Dorothy tried to accept this as typical teen behavior, but Jenny's transformation was beyond the norm. The most alarming change was Jenny's animosity toward her mother and her physical and emotional deterioration. Jenny seemed possessed, often cursing and ranting at Dorothy. Any signs of her love and compassion had disappeared, replaced by bitterness and hostility. Dorothy had divorced Jenny's father five years earlier, and now her daughter seized on that, saying she was mistreated and neglected by her parents. Dorothy felt defenseless against Jenny's tirades.

When Dorothy overheard Jenny in a phone conversation referring to "huffers" and "E," and making other references that appeared to be about drugs, Dorothy confronted her daughter. Jenny screamed obscenities, telling her to stay out of her business, and then stormed out of the house. Soon, mother and daughter communicated with each other mostly through rage. Dorothy could not understand how Jenny could make such self-destructive choices. *How could she create this pain and suffering?* she wondered. *How could she be so selfish?*

Mother and daughter circled each other like enemies at war. They became so alienated from each other that Dorothy caught herself wishing that the drugs would just kill this stranger, this devil in her child's body. Dorothy was exhausted.

Instead of sleeping, she sat up night after night trying to think of a way to reclaim her lost daughter. Should she press charges and throw her daughter in jail? Should she call her ex-husband, who lived 500 miles away, and risk hearing yet again that she was a bad mother and didn't deserve to have custody? Counseling had failed, so she was reluctant to call the therapist and be reminded of all the mistakes she had allegedly made as a single mother. She wondered if she should call the doctor who had prescribed Ritalin for the ADHD (attention deficit hyperactivity disorder) Jenny had been diagnosed with after the divorce.

✦ ✦

The phone rang at 4:27 the morning after Dorothy discovered that Jenny had taken valuables from their home. Dorothy didn't recognize the number.

"Hello, ma'am, is this Dorothy Fredrick?"

"Yes, it is," she replied, exhausted and brokenhearted.

"This is Sergeant Roberts with Police Headquarters." The report was worse than Dorothy had ever feared possible. Sergeant Roberts said Jenny had been in a car headed the wrong way down a highway when her car collided head-on with a minivan carrying a family of five. Three members of the family were killed. Only the father and his three-year-old daughter were clinging to life.

Jenny was in the county hospital with only minor injuries, but she might be charged with drug intoxication and as an accessory to vehicular homicide. Sergeant Roberts explained that she had been high on drugs, engaging in oral sex with the driver at the time of the crash.

Dorothy was so stunned she could barely speak. She thanked the officer weakly and hung up, and then she began to notify family members that her daughter's downward spiral had sunk to a horrifying low, beyond anything she could have imagined.

Eventually, Jenny came to my clinic as a patient. She was aware of her self-destructive actions and the pain she was inflicting on those who loved her, but the drugs had mastery over her and her value system. They cured the emotional pain she felt—but only temporarily. Jenny felt terrible about what she had become, assailing herself as an insult to her family, as a slut, whore, liar, and "a complete and total waste of life."

Jenny's addiction and sexual promiscuity took a heavy toll on her mind, body, and spirit, endangering her ability to have children—and her very life. She had turned predatory, willing to use or attack anyone to procure her drugs and feed her addiction. When Jenny came to us as a patient, we provided her with in-depth therapy that helped her find peace and resolve most of her challenges. Jenny's story is one of thousands that we've encountered at our recovery center in recent years. Some of those cases ended with miraculous transformations, thanks to many of the methods revealed in this book. In the most extreme cases, however, the addict sank to a level beyond our reach.

Addiction Has Many Victims

Alcohol and drug addiction have reached epidemic proportions in the United States and many other nations. While most treatment programs focus on the addicted person, it's not only the addict who needs help and compassion. Spouses, partners, parents, siblings, grandparents, and other family and friends suffer as a result of addiction. In Jenny's case and far too many others, innocent victims are killed, injured, or emotionally scarred at the hands of the addict.

Statistics tell us that many millions of people around the world are affected in one way or another by the disease of addiction, which is defined as any obsession that causes harm. This can include a sugar obsession that turns into the disease of diabetes, an addiction to fatty foods that eventually clogs the arteries and causes heart failure, or an addiction to plastic surgery that ends with disastrous infections. Although drug and alcohol addiction is more prevalent in males, females are certainly not immune. In fact, women with drug and alcohol addictions often incur far worse problems than males.

Historical and Current-Day Perspectives

We know that drugs and alcohol have been used for pleasure and anxiety relief since early in human history. Fermented beverages appeared as early as the Neolithic period, around 10,000 B.C. Some historians think beer was a human food staple before bread. Archaeologists have documented wine production depicted in Egyptian art as far back as 4000 B.C. Narcotic use was noted around the same period. Overindulgence and addiction follow the same historical path.

The enactment of Prohibition in 1920 restricted the use of alcohol on a national scale because of concern that alcohol abuse was a threat to the moral fiber of society and a catalyst for crime, violence, disease, and the break-down of traditional family structure. After Prohibition went into effect, the costs associated with the same problems grew even greater. Criminal-operated distill-eries, breweries, and speakeasies flourished. Thus, there was a general sense of relief when President Roosevelt presented the repeal of Prohibition in 1933, making the production and consumption of alcohol legal once again in the U.S.

The United States has had an anti–drug abuse pro-gram since the late 1980s. The goal is to wipe out ille-gal drug use, manufacturing, and trafficking, as well as drug-related crimes, violence, and related health threats. Although the federal government has poured more than $340 million into drug prevention and antidrug law en-forcement in recent years, the new programs will likely be no more successful than Prohibition in putting an end to the addiction epidemic in the U.S.

One reason is the ever-growing increase in the num-ber of people addicted to medically prescribed drugs, one of the deadliest forms of addiction. The number of prescriptions for depression, pain, and anxiety drugs has skyrocketed in the past decade. Those three health con-cerns are generally treated with prescription drugs that are often abused and lead to addiction. Consider the story one of my patients, who had been diagnosed with lupus. Her doctor prescribed pain medication to deal with her immense discomfort from rheumatoid arthri-tis and muscle and back pains. The medication helped initially, but then her tolerance for pain decreased, caus-ing even greater suffering. She took more and more pain medication until she reached an almost catatonic state.

Her brother found her one day, lying naked in a pool of vomit and dead from an overdose. She was 23 years old.

I am not the only therapist or social commentator to conclude that society has become overreliant on "magic pills." The explosion in pharmaceuticals has triggered a corresponding explosion in abuse and addiction—and the problem is not limited to prescription drugs. Currently, more than 300 plants can be synthesized and sold (either by prescription or by illegal means) as stimulants, depressants, or hallucinogens to treat anxiety and pain. Most drugs go by different names, depending upon which neighborhood you live in. (See Appendix B for the variety of names assigned to the top 20.)

The recent boom in over-the-counter "bath salts" sold in gas stations and truck stops is just one example. Ingesting these products, most of which are made by illegal labs, can lead to extreme agitation, paranoia, anxiety, hallucinations, and dangerously erratic behavior. This explosion in "recreational" and street drugs is a threat that cannot be reversed merely by law enforcement and the courts. So many of these illicit drugs come and go that it's almost impossible to stay on top of them. Emergency-room doctors are saying they can't keep up with treatments, either.

Daily marijuana use increased among 8th, 10th, and 12th graders from 2009 to 2010, paralleling softening attitudes about the risk associated with using marijuana among teenagers, even as cigarette smoking has declined, according to the 2010 Monitoring the Future (MTF) survey conducted by the University of Michigan's Institute for Social Research. The survey also found increased usage and acceptance of prescription and over-the-counter medications by teenagers. Among the most-abused medications mentioned in the survey: Oxycontin, Adderall, Ecstasy, and over-the-counter cough and cold medicines.

There's always a price to pay for each addictive substance, even the most common and socially accepted drugs of choice: nicotine and alcohol. Nicotine brings with it the well-documented threat of cancer, not to mention lung and heart damage. Long-term alcohol abuse can result in major brain dysfunction, as well as cirrhosis of the liver, pancreatitis, epilepsy, polyneuropathy, alcoholic dementia, nutritional deficiencies, damage to the central and peripheral nervous systems, and sexual dysfunction. Other physical effects include an increased risk of developing cardiovascular disease, alcoholic liver disease, and cancer.

Women alcoholics have a higher mortality rate from alcoholism than men and an increased risk of breast cancer. Additionally, heavy drinking over time has been found to have a negative effect on reproductive functions in women, which means decreased ovarian mass, problems with or irregularity of the menstrual cycle, and early menopause.

Today, the U.S. addiction treatment industry is expected to have revenues of $34 billion by 2014, an increase of 55 percent from 2005, according to a 2011 report by DailyFinance.com. According to the report, all but 20 percent of the cost is underwritten by public funding; the rest is covered by insurance or private funds. The costs of drug rehabilitation are far from standardized. Rehab centers that cater to the rich and famous are known to charge as much as $100,000 for a month of private rooms and private physicians. A one-month stay at Hazelden, one of the country's oldest and most respected facilities, costs $28,500. Outpatient programs run closer to $10,000 a month.

The collateral damage that accompanies addiction is often beyond measure because of the impact on family members, loved ones, friends, co-workers, and businesses. Everyone feels the pain directly or indirectly. Those in closest contact with addicts commonly suffer shame and depression. The addiction poisons interpersonal relationships and can even delay the development of social skills in younger family members. Loved ones also often suffer bankruptcy and other serious financial problems either due to the irresponsible actions of the addict or because of legal and medical costs. The ripple effect likely touches millions and millions more worldwide.

Not all drug addicts have car crashes and kill others, but many leave a tragic trail of devastated lives and broken homes. Addiction has no prejudice. Black, brown, or white; rich or poor, this evil force preys upon all with equal malevolence. Addicts have only one route to access joy. The drug of choice becomes an obsession, which becomes a physical disease.

What Isn't Working in Addiction Treatment

The standard Western approach to addiction, particularly alcoholism and drug addiction, is to punish addicts as criminals rather than provide help for them as victims of disease. Since intoxication is not considered a defense for criminal actions, addicts who break laws while under the influence are usually jailed on criminal charges in the United States. Some nations are even more severe in their treatment of addicts. But as witnessed by Prohibition in the United States during the 1920s as well as by our present-day antidrug policies, the legal system and its punitive measures have not eliminated addiction as a major societal problem.

General psychiatry has not enjoyed much success in treating addiction. Simply talking to patients about their addiction works with only about 15 percent of the treatable addict population because so many addicts have difficulty communicating and comprehending. The brain of a drug-addicted person can take at least two years to fully heal from the toxicities and destruction of drug use—and psychology counseling isn't likely to have a lasting impact until such individuals function at minimal cognitive levels, which includes the ability to make reasoned choices.

Another challenge is the resistance against defining addiction as a physical disease rather than a mental disease—an issue of contention within the scientific community. Another factor is the "wall" between psychiatrists and drug-addiction counselors. Many psychiatrists attempt to treat drug addiction with prescription medication, while many licensed drug-addiction counselors see this as simply trading one addiction for another.

Addicts need access to treatment and counseling around the clock. Alcoholics Anonymous (AA) and similar organizations provide such access, but most psychologists in private practice cannot. The only consistent program with any record of success in treating addiction is commonly known as the 12-step program, which is used by AA. The majority of treatment programs in the United States follow the 12 steps, introduced by AA co-founders Bill Wilson and Dr. Bob Smith in 1935. Millions of recovering addicts credit the 12-step program as a major factor in their efforts to achieve sobriety.

Recidivism rates for those who go through drug- and alcohol-treatment programs are amazingly high. Most professionals believe the majority of addicts must go through treatment programs over and over until they finally stop using drugs or alcohol. My clinical experience shows that each addict must find the specific treatment that works for him or her. An effective treatment for addiction is one that allows each person to return to health, in whatever way works for that individual. This is true of any program, whether it is for cancer, chronic pain, cardiovascular rehabilitation, weight management, or addiction.

I know many dedicated and self-sacrificing drug- and alcohol-addiction counselors. Most do great work. I work beside several great counselors on a daily basis. My comments are not meant as criticism of them or their profession. Instead, I am making observations about the limits of one-dimensional programs. AA's own data states that 64 percent of addicts drop out of AA in their first year, which leads me to the conclusion that AA is not the program for everyone.

Interesting enough, insurance companies are adopting more "evidence-based therapies" and not paying for the 12-step program without concurrent treatments. There is a strong movement by insurers to integrate AA's faith-based program into more measurable processes. With more than 11,000 rehab centers in the United States, and especially with the changes occurring in federal health programs and specifications, determining the best and most effective treatment isn't a simple process.

New Cause for Hope

So far, I have not offered much in the way of hope. I'm about to change that, but I want you to understand that the time to act is now. You can't simply hope that your addicted teen will snap out of it. An addict isn't going through a phase or self-medicating to deal with a temporary issue. The problem that spurred the drug or alcohol abuse may go away, but the addiction will not. I'm about to present a no-nonsense approach that will strengthen your child as well as the total family structure while arming you with defenses against those who manufacture, market, and distribute addictive drugs.

Today's teenagers and 20-somethings have far more "downtime" than previous generations of young people. Because so many parents must work, teens now often spend more time without supervision than teens of past decades. They watch more television and more movies and videos. They also have easy access to the Internet, which can be a tremendous resource but which is also rife with dangerous and bad information that many young people are incapable of sorting from the truth.

We have become a "get more" society, wanting more and more for less effort. Too many people want a "magic pill" to offset boredom, depression, anxiety, and loneliness. Far too many parents have abandoned their responsibilities to discipline and guide their children. Instead, it's not uncommon for parents to give their children drugs to keep them under control.

I believe the family can play a far more significant role in prevention and care for addicts. I have seen teenagers turn their lives around without rehab. A home "treatment" can work and is certainly less costly than the alternative—but it does take considerable effort.

My program involving family and home treatment is a strong and effective approach. This book will serve as a manual for parents and others dealing with an addicted loved one in the preteen and teenage years. Consider your involvement in this program an investment in your child's health and well-being and in the future of your family.

I will offer you an action plan so that you can apply this innovative approach in the real world. The process will require a concerted effort, some prayer, and a lot of love, as well as ample doses of tough love, common sense, and a willingness to face the consequences. You can love your child and hate the addiction that has tortured your relationship. Even the teen with no drug or alcohol problems can be a handful because of hormonal urges, the quest for independence, and a still-maturing brain rewiring itself. If you are among those parents who have long feared your child's teen years, take heart in the fact that you are not alone. This is natural.

When I conduct surveys through the *Dr. Phil* network, 95 percent of parents express concerns about the teen years, even if their child is only two years old. A lot of this ambivalence is understandable and attributable to the parents' own experiences as teens, not to mention the understandable dread of dealing with teenage rebelliousness.

While this book offers no magic cure for the typical teen torment most parents encounter, I will offer specific and proven advice for the parent dealing with a preteen, teen, or young adult who has become addicted to drugs or alcohol. I assure you, without hesitation, that you can get through this trying and sometimes heart-wrenching challenge. The experience may even teach you something valuable about yourself, your child, and the power of unconditional love.

Treatments Based on the Science of Brain Plasticity

Many of the normal parental frustrations that arise during a child's teenage years stem from natural and necessary changes that take place inside the maturing teenage brain. Your teenager's ability to gauge risk, to weigh the consequences of actions, to control impulses, and to think long-term are all affected by a teenage brain that is rewiring—breaking old connections and making new ones.

The brain's ability to form new neural connections throughout life is called *neuroplasticity.* This amazing capability is what allows the brain's nerve cells (neurons) to adjust and compensate for injuries or disease. You have probably heard of cases in which one side or hemisphere of the brain is damaged due to an injury and the other hemisphere compensates by reorganizing and forming new connections between undamaged neurons.

In my work with an innovative drug rehabilitation and recovery program in South Texas, we have found ways to tap into the brain's amazing powers of reorganization. The most effective methods come from a combination of modern and ancient medicines and technologies that heal the brain and allow a teenager to grow more responsive and more capable of making good choices.

Our method only works if the patient and those around the individual are committed to recovery and rehabilitation. Motivation is the most critical element of recovery, which encompasses both mental and spiritual aspects, as I'll discuss throughout the upcoming chapters.

✦ ✦ ✦

CHAPTER ONE

SOCIAL SOURCES OF TEENAGE ADDICTION AND ALCOHOL- AND DRUG-ABUSE BELIEFS

Parents dealing with addicted children are often confused about what constitutes addiction and how a child reaches that state. Many times a father (or a mother) will say that he used alcohol and drugs as a teenager without falling into addiction. "I came out okay," he might say. "So what's wrong with my son? Are kids today just soft—or has society changed? What's the harm if a kid goes out in his first year in college and has a few drinking binges?"

It's true: people, and particularly teenagers, have been altering their state of consciousness with alcohol and drugs since the dawn of humans. So what constitutes "normal" and "safe" drug use, and what constitutes abuse and addiction?

The answers depend on each person's personal history. Why is the teenager drinking in the first place? I have some strong thoughts on these issues because I don't see many cases where a child just straightens out upon reaching maturity in his or her mid-20s. What I do see in our clinic are people with severe addictions who are in desperate need of care. Counter to what you may hear, there are no medications that cure addictions. Recovery requires maximum effort by both the addict and those who want the addict to be cured.

According to the American Society of Addiction Medicine, addiction is a primary, chronic disease of brain reward, motivation, memory, and elated circuitry. Addiction is characterized by the inability to consistently abstain from a substance, impairment in behavioral control, cravings, and diminished recognition of significant problems with one's dysfunctional relationships. Without treatment or recovery, addiction is progressive and can result in disability or premature death. Both prescription as well as recreational drug use can lead to addiction.

Prescribed Drug Usage

The use of medications for treating children has reached levels that some characterize as "epidemic." One drug far-too-often prescribed is Adderall, used to treat ADHD. Few realize that Adderall, a popular study aid on college campuses, is a stimulant that the U.S. Drug Enforcement Administration places in the same class as cocaine. In my opinion, too many doctors write a prescription for Adderall when a young person claims to have trouble focusing on schoolwork, meeting deadlines, or being organized.

As you can imagine, those symptoms fit the complaints of many people—but since insurance companies don't pay for more complex diagnostics to determine if the symptoms are true ADHD, most doctors don't order more thorough tests. Although estimates of how often this condition is misdiagnosed vary, the bottom line is that many children are taking medication for ADHD that they may not actually need.

One of our patients, Dick, was diagnosed with ADHD at the age of five and was immediately placed on Adderall. He remained on this drug until he went to college, when he quit on his own. He began using the drug again, however, becoming convinced that it helped him get better grades because he could study longer and with more focus. Like a performance-enhancing drug used by an athlete, Adderall enhances academic performance. Dick told his doctors he couldn't keep his grades up without it. When he couldn't get a prescription from a physician, he turned to the thriving black market for the drug on campus.

Heavy use of Adderall and other stimulants can trigger depression, which is exactly what happened to Dick. Tragically, he went into a rapid downward spiral that led to him taking his own life before he could get adequate help from loved ones or professionals.

Dick's case is all too common. Prescription medications can become addictive and trigger depression as well as high-risk behaviors. Pain medications, stimulants, and anxiety modifiers are among the prescription medications that can be addictive both psychologically and biologically. Prescription drugs can also cause serious problems when taken with other medications, such as drugs for weight control and hormone management.

Pills Are Not a Substitute for Parenting

Far too many parents accept prescription drugs as a means to control their children's behavioral problems because they believe it is easier to drug a child than to develop the necessary parenting skills or to work through a child's issues with professional counseling. Child psychologists are concerned that children today have fewer outlets for creativity and high energy because they are less active physically and spend more time engaged in sedentary activities, such as playing video games, surfing the Internet, and watching videos or television. They believe such children aren't learning socialization skills or how to manage their own emotions and impulses.

Another concern is that in most cases, a child who is given prescription medication for behavioral problems is simply being numbed emotionally. This stunts development and can serve as a gateway to addiction. The child learns to see drugs as a quick fix—a primary reason the black market in Adderall and Ritalin (another drug commonly prescribed for ADHD) is booming on campuses across the U.S.

Teenagers fortunate enough to receive professional help can overcome addiction through a detox program, but even then the teen must learn how to deal with future behavioral and emotional issues without returning to addictive drugs. Teenagers who have been numbed at a young age don't have the same level of maturity as their drug-free peers. An addicted teenager often must be placed in a supervised program to find other more emotionally intelligent methods for coping with stress, anxiety, and impulsive behaviors. Many such programs are available, including wilderness-oriented programs, rehab programs, and equine-therapy programs. Parents and other family members often participate in these programs, because once the program is completed, the addicted teenager will need a loving support group with solid relationships.

Recreational Drug Use

It's widely believed that the younger a brain is, the more destruction drug and alcohol abuse cause. Consider the case of Cris, a girl who was raised in an alcoholic family. From the age of 13, Cris would sit in the garage with her father, drinking vodka and discussing his troubled relationship with her mother. Not surprisingly, Cris became an addict. Her father's inappropriate behavior left her with distorted views on relationships, conflict resolution, and parenting.

Cris's whole development—biological, psychological, and spiritual—was stunted. Teens who start drinking by age 13 have a 43 percent chance of becoming an alcoholic, compared to only a 10 percent chance for a person who begins drinking at age 21, according to the Genetic Science Learning Center at the University of Utah. Another disturbing statistic: the average age patients at the Origins Recovery Centers in Texas started drinking alcohol is 12 years old.

During adolescence, the brain goes through a pruning exercise described in detail in Chapter 3. Through this neurological development phase, young people often have feelings of dissociation and "being different" or isolated that cause them to question where they fit in and what their purpose and value might be. This state of mind causes stress. During this period, parents and guardians need to take an active role in being supportive and keeping lines of communication open. Giving children tools to build emotional intelligence at this time is also critical for their emotional, intellectual, and spiritual development.

Drinking numbs emotions, so teenagers who consume alcohol and drugs suffer both emotional as well as biological consequences. Numbing emotions can lead to feelings of depersonalization, along with a release of inhibitions that can result in unleashed anger and other self-destructive emotions. Addiction sets in when there is psychological dependence on drugs or alcohol and a teenager loses the ability to deal with typical adolescent feelings and questions.

Teen marijuana use is at its highest in 30 years, and teens are now more likely to use marijuana than tobacco, according to the American Academy of Child & Adolescent Psychiatry. In 2011, a national study showed that one in eight 8th graders, one in four 10th graders, and one in three 12th graders have used marijuana in the past year. Like alcohol, pot also has the effect of numbing emotions and sensations, which can cause stress and disorientation in the still-developing teenage brain. In many cases, teenagers who smoke pot lose their ability to make good decisions. Those who do so after the age of 21 are less likely to suffer from this because their brains are more developed.

Binge Drinking

One of the major contributors to teenage alcohol addiction is the practice of binge drinking, which often occurs during drinking games such as the popular "beer pong," in which participants chug cups of beer. The popularity of doing shots of vodka, tequila, bourbon, and other potent liquor also contributes to college-age binge drinking. Parents and guardians should explain the dangers and potential long-term impact of binge drinking to their teenagers.

Underage drinkers consume more than 90 percent of their alcohol by binge drinking, according to the National Institute on Alcohol Abuse and Alcoholism (NIAAA). Binge drinking is defined as having at least three drinks for girls or three to five drinks for boys (depending on their age) within a two-hour time period, creating a blood-alcohol level of .08 or higher. NIAAA stats show that 6.9 million young people report having five or more drinks on the same occasion, within a few hours, at least once in the past month. Equally disturbing is that 93.4 percent of adolescents ages 12 to 14 who drank alcohol in the past month got it for free—in many cases, getting it through relatives or finding it at home.

While binge drinking may be a response to other problems for many teenagers, it is also a common expression of general adolescent turmoil. Binge drinking, often beginning around age 13, tends to increase during adolescence, peak during young adulthood (ages 18 to 22), then gradually decrease. Individuals who increase their binge drinking from age 18 to 24, and those who consistently binge drink at least once a week during this period, may have problems navigating life's challenges during the transition from adolescence to young adulthood. The damage alcohol abuse does to the brain and to emotional development during this time may result in difficulty in relationships, studies, employment, and finances.

Parental Responsibilities

Most teenagers are seeking answers to their problems, either consciously or subconsciously. For that reason, it is critical that parents keep lines of communication open and remain actively engaged in monitoring their children's behavior during these critical teenage years when young people are so vulnerable due to their still-developing brains. It's a challenge, I know, because teenagers tend to think parents are clueless, and they typically reject their advice.

Don't take it personally—but don't accept the rejection and rebellion. If you're a parent, you have a responsibility to protect and guide your children. Failing to fulfill that responsibility may result in lifelong problems for your teenager. You can't be the child's parent and the child's best friend at the same time. In truth, most teenagers are looking for parental guidelines to help them make the right decisions, even if they seem to reject that guidance.

Scientists and psychologists don't agree on the exact point when alcohol or drug abuse escalates into addiction. Many factors are involved and each individual is different, but remember what students often say in college fraternity houses: drinking is a problem when it's a problem. In my counseling sessions, parents of teenagers struggling with addiction or drug and alcohol abuse often ask, "How do you parent, guide, heal, or simply communicate with a teenager who is focused mostly on texting, tweeting, surfing the Internet, or e-mailing friends?" In the chapters that follow, I offer guidance and suggestions addressing that critical concern.

✦ ✦ ✦

CHAPTER TWO

Early Detection of Addictive Behaviors in Teenagers

Addiction is a disease. As with any illness, the earlier you can detect it, the better. Not everyone is an addict, regardless of how much one experiments with drugs and alcohol. Many teenagers drink socially without becoming alcoholics. Many experiment with marijuana without moving on to more serious drugs.

Still, parents need to monitor their teenagers because social drinking and occasional marijuana use can accelerate quickly. You don't have to actually catch your child with drugs or drug paraphernalia to know that something is up. Look for these early indicators of drug and alcohol abuse:

- Extreme mood changes, especially from cynicism to anger, including hair-trigger emotions that demonstrate a lack of inhibition of emotions in the brain

- Quick anger when suspected of being under the influence

- Violent and verbally abusive behavior

- Loud and obnoxious behavior unsuited to social situations, or silent and withdrawn behavior in social settings

- Infantile, passive-aggressive, and manipulative behavior

- Extreme shifts in sleeping patterns (teenagers need a lot of sleep, but a teen using drugs or alcohol will be extreme in both sleep needs and excessive levels of energy)

- Obvious deception and conflicting stories (which are the result of a brain operating in pure "pleasure-seeking" mode because of the addictive cravings)

- Dilated pupils (a symptom of the brain attempting to stabilize perceptions of reality)

- Drastic weight loss or gain (unexplained weight loss can be due to the use of stimulants, such as methamphetamine or cocaine; weight gain can be related to the use of depressants, such as pot, alcohol, or even heroin)

- Signs of stealing, usually for drug money

- Hanging out with new friends who are also drug users

- Paranoid moods and perceived sense of persecution by a "conspiracy" of the family, old friends, law enforcement, or anyone trying to stop addictive behavior and drug use

- Concerns expressed by siblings, friends, classmates, teachers, coaches, spiritual advisors, or others close to the teenager that "something seems wrong" with the teenager's behavior

Symptoms of Drug/Alcohol Dependency

In the medical world, signs and symptoms help doctors diagnose a disease. In the event that an addicted teenager admits to drug abuse, these measures can be helpful in determining the level of dependency:

- Uses increased quantities
- Hides use (uses alone)
- Uses away from home
- Can't stop
- Increases occasions of intoxication

Assessment of Enabling by Parents

While it is obvious that the teenager is the focus of early detection and treatment for addiction, in some cases parents subconsciously serve as enablers. When discussing chemical dependency, the term *enabler* takes on a very negative meaning. An enabler is a person around the teenager who steps in to protect unhealthy, irresponsible, and antisocial behavior and who saves the teenager from the fate of suffering consequences. Here is a test for parents to highlight enabling behaviors or attitudes:

1. Do you try to sweep aside your belief that your teenager is abusing drugs and is probably chemically dependent?

2. Do you usually keep your feelings about being a parent to yourself in order to protect your child's feelings?

3. Do you avoid problems because you hope that issues will resolve themselves and because you want to keep peace?

4. Do you believe that conflict is a problem in and of itself?

5. Do you delay acting on problems by thinking, *It's not so bad, and things will get better when my teenager grows up?*

6. Do you try to protect your child from the pain and stigma related to addiction?

7. Do you often take over your child's responsibilities to make things work out?

8. Do you feel that you alone know what is best for your child?

9. Do you tend to be controlling?

10. Do you wait for a "higher power" or force to come to the rescue?

11. Do you lecture, blame, or criticize your teenager for chemical dependency?

12. Do you secretly do things for your teenager or give money to "help"?

13. Have you given your child multiple chances for redemption without requiring accountability for past transgressions?

14. Are you afraid that without your supervision your child will sink deeper into addiction?

If you answered "yes" to more than a couple of these questions, it is likely you are on some level an enabling parent and part of the problem. For a time, enabling may prevent social conflict and financial difficulties for the family. However, by ignoring the problem and delaying treatment, addiction is prolonged, often putting both child and parents in increasing danger.

Enablers may act out of a sincere sense of love, loyalty, and concern. The major motivation for enablers, regardless of behavior, is usually a deep caring for the addicted teenager. Sometimes enablers are motivated out of shame, or fear of being held responsible. Parents and other concerned people may see no alternatives because they simply do not understand addiction and chemical dependency. Enabling can quickly turn into all-out denial.

You are enabling and even reinforcing addictive behavior if you are covering up for a teenager, making excuses, doing homework or chores, or ignoring irresponsible behavior. These are signs that you are caught up in the illness—and may be unwittingly contributing to the problem.

Teenage "Types," Their Characteristics— and Intervention Opportunities

Some individuals are genetically predisposed to addictive behaviors, and some are emotionally more vulnerable. In my experience, there are "teenage types" who are more at risk for addiction than most, and if your child fits into one of those described below, you should be particularly alert to changes in behavior and other warning signs. I recommend professional guidance if you have questions or concerns beyond what is addressed here.

Type A Teenagers

Fourth-grader Sandy was motivated and goal oriented. She had high hopes for success as both a gymnast and as a singer. Her father was supportive, but he also pressured Sandy to get straight A's along with perfecting her gymnast routines and singing.

Like many children today, Sandy learned early on from her classmates that the psycho-stimulant Adderall, often prescribed for ADHD, helps with focus as well as weight control. At first, Sandy took the drug with a doctor's prescription, obtained by her mother. But Sandy soon became psychologically dependent on the medication.

Sandy felt her grades and performance as an athlete and singer would suffer if she did not take Adderall. Sandy did have success as a gymnast, gaining recognition for her skills, but as she grew older, she began taking other drugs in hopes that they would further enhance her performance and relieve the stress and anxiety that came with intense competition. As an adult, Sandy developed a cocaine addiction. She went to rehab several times without lasting success. Thankfully, she met a minister who succeeded in awakening her to the dangers of addiction. He set her on a path to recovery.

While Adderall and Ritalin are both stimulants successfully prescribed to counter hyperactivity and attention deficit disorders, evidence shows that students, from elementary schools to colleges and universities, are using these drugs to help them focus on their studies. This is like taking steroids for the brain. Adderall and Ritalin are performance-enhancing drugs, and they've been adopted by young people under pressure. Some students make the case to their parents that if they don't use these drugs, they'll be at a disadvantage compared to those classmates who do use them.

Young people have become quite savvy in feigning ADHD in order to get prescriptions from family doctors. There are several dangers in this development, not the least of which is the widespread belief that drugs are a solution for most of life's challenges. Young people need to learn to function and thrive by developing problem-solving skills instead of simply by popping pills.

I've seen parents of young athletes giving their sons and daughters drugs to enhance performance and curb their appetite, a dangerous practice that can stunt growth, interfere with natural body processes, and lead to serious medical and psychological problems. Parents need to teach their children to take personal responsibility instead of encouraging drug reliance.

Characteristics of type A teenagers

- Having a narrow concept of success
- Having a "do-whatever-it-takes" life philosophy
- No understanding of the "enjoy-the-journey" philosophy

Interventions for addicted type A teenagers

Since type A children are often the product of type A parents, adults must model balanced and healthy behaviors. In other words, if the parents are all about winning and being the absolute best, the teenager will mirror that behavior—or rebel against it. The following interventions may be helpful:

- Help redefine success in ways that encourage healthier lifestyles.
- Encourage more balance, with less emphasis on being number one and more emphasis on enjoying life and pursuing passions.

Spirit Teenagers

Ann was 25 years old before she finally took control of a life dominated by addiction. She had been prostituting herself to support her heroin addiction. She almost died twice from hepatitis and severe infections after she'd broken off needles in her arm while injecting herself with the drug.

Ann had been a gifted and sensitive child. As a teenager, she brought homeless people to her parents' kitchen and fed them. While it may seem odd that such an empathetic child would turn to drugs, it is not uncommon for highly sensitive people to become reliant on drugs to help them deal with vulnerabilities. They learn to use drugs as a shield against the hatred and evil they see in the world, choosing to dissociate and retreat into a magical land because their sensitivity makes dealing with the darker side of humanity painful. I call such highly spiritual and highly sensitive people "spirit children."

Characteristics of spirit teenagers

- Having high levels of empathy for others
- Showing early interest in spiritual and religious topics
- Showing early signs of spinning around in circles to achieve an altered state of consciousness
- Tending to withdraw and dissociate from unpleasant situations and events
- Displaying a strong sense of justice and fairness
- Bringing home stray and injured animals

Interventions for addicted spirit teenagers

Although this driven personality type may well self-correct before addiction sets in, these intervention methods may prove helpful:

- Encourage relaxation techniques through meditation, remote imagery, biofeedback, and intensive prayer circles.

- Encourage participation in healing-imagery groups and celebrative rituals.

- Discuss spiritual matters and the power of faith and love.

- Encourage journaling about experiences.

- Encourage the exploration of nature and investigate the beauty and interconnectedness of all creatures.

- Provide opportunities for expression through music and using music as a source of relaxation and stimulation.

Dangerously Bored Teenagers

John was extremely bright as a child. He knew his multiplication tables before his peers, and at age nine he was writing letters to his congressman. Early in his school years he was an avid and engaged student—but his interest in classes diminished because he had trouble by the time he was eight making friends with classmates who generally weren't as bright.

John became bored with schoolwork and socially isolated. He turned to drugs for his "learning" experiences. Eventually, he developed a cocaine addiction and supported his habit by robbing elderly women of their purses and stealing jewelry and other valuables from homes in blue-collar and middle-class neighborhoods.

John had a superiority complex. He believed he was above the law and that most rules and regulations did not apply to him. He was skilled at manipulating the legal system, and when the courts showed him leniency, it only made him more contemptuous.

In this case, John's boredom and contempt proved fatal. His cocaine addiction eventually became cocaine psychosis. He was convinced that the CIA was reading his mind. Tragically, John died by driving off a bridge in Big Sur, California.

Characteristics of dangerously bored teenagers

- Performing poorly in school despite evidence of a good mind

- Displaying improper humor and social awkwardness

- Having few friends among peers and classmates

- Having a tendency to spend too much time engaged in solitary activities, playing video games, going to movies, and eating alone

Interventions for addicted dangerously bored teenagers

The dangerously bored teenager is often bright, socially inept, and convinced that most rules do not apply to him. The secret to dealing with these teenagers is to keep their minds engaged in constructive activities and to help them socialize with peers who will be good influences. The following interventions may help:

- Encourage advanced learning programs, hobbyist groups, and other programs that might involve computers, media technology, and engineering and science.

- Suggest sports and physical activity, which can help engage individuals who tend to be loners; track, cross-country, wrestling, tennis, rock climbing, and outdoor programs such as Outward Bound are all good choices.

- Advocate programs that use music and rhythm, such as dance teams and drumming exercises, to encourage increased creativity and engagement in school.

Lonely Teenagers

Jill was a loner as a child, in part because her family had moved ten times. She avoided her classmates for fear of being teased or rejected. Unfortunately, the friends she did make were from a bad crowd: a particularly rebellious group of "Goths," who dressed in black clothing and wore severe makeup. While not all Goths are troublemakers, this particular group was overly defiant, unruly, and secretive. They demanded that Jill pledge her loyalty to their group, so she got facial piercings. They were also drug users—and Jill joined them in that. Her grades deteriorated, and like her new friends, she did the bare minimum to stay in school. Jill lost all ambition and fell into a life of drug abuse and constant struggle.

Characteristics of lonely teenagers

- Being a loner or hanging out with other outcasts and outsiders
- Dressing in extreme styles, obtaining multiple piercings and tattoos, and experimenting with extreme hairstyles and colors, all of which may indicate a struggle with identity and socialization issues
- Losing interest in school and performing at the minimum level
- Showing disdain for family activities, and not taking part in meals and family discussions

Interventions for addicted lonely teenagers

Lonely teenagers need to learn to be part of groups that support healthy behavior. The following are a few suggestions to start getting them back on track:

- Help them break ties to cliques of antisocial outsiders and drug users.

- Help them rebuild family ties.

- Urge them to associate with a healthier crowd of friends.

- Put in for a transfer to new school.

- Encourage participation in sports teams or clubs.

Risk-Taking or ADHD Teenagers

This type of individual is particularly prone to drug and alcohol addiction. I've worked with many risk takers and ADHD teenagers (often they are both), including Wade, a handsome and ambitious 14-year-old with a bright smile. In conversation, Wade appeared to be deeply engaged, although his mind was usually a thousand miles away. His lack of engagement had nothing to do with being bored or having antisocial tendencies. In fact, sometimes Wade would snap back and suddenly become attentive—but then his eyes would glaze over again and you could tell his mind was wandering once more.

Wade's tendency to get lost in a "fog" resulted in him failing eighth grade. This was particularly devastating because his friends would be moving on to high school, and Wade would be left behind to complete his last year of middle school. He became listless, sullen, and withdrawn. Soon he had labeled himself as "dumb." Wade said his problems in school were due to a mind "that never seems to stop."

"It's like trying to watch a dozen TV shows at once," he described. "And I can't follow the story line of any of them! It's not like I'm not trying to prioritize and stay focused on one thing at a time. But I never can. I just go from one thing to another, trying to understand as much as I can as I go along. I'm such a loser."

Wade's challenges led him to self-medicate. By the age of 15, he was addicted to "uppers." The amphetamines at first actually helped him calm his mind and allowed him to concentrate on his studies while taming his restlessness. Unfortunately, as often happens, he overmedicated and his problems deepened. He was in and out of rehab five times before he simply disappeared. I have not heard if his family ever tracked him down, and I fear that he is now either homeless or worse.

The most recent research on ADHD tells us that the frontal lobes of ADHD children often are performing at low levels. This is the part of the brain responsible for the cognitive functions of organization and planning. As a result, these children often instinctively seek stimulation to "wake up" their brains to snap out of the dreamy "fog" described by Wade and many others afflicted with ADHD. We sometimes call this an ADHD "brain storm," or brain stress pattern.

To make things worse, in those with ADHD, the brain's pleasure centers (the accumbens) metabolize glucose (energy food for the brain) at about 50 percent below normal levels. So it makes sense that Wade felt "normal" when he was on an amphetamine high, because the pleasure centers were being stimulated. As often happens, though, the self-medicating ADHD sufferer becomes driven to find more and more stimulation, which leads to more powerful and more addictive drugs (such as cocaine). Wade followed that path in his quest to "be normal." It is a dangerous path that often leads to tragedy.

Characteristics of risk-taking or ADHD teenagers

- Being bored with life
- Having difficulty focusing on one task or topic; poor recollection
- Having difficulty following directions
- Performing poorly on tests that require sustained concentration
- Frequently failing to finish projects
- Acting irresponsibly
- Having difficulty organizing or prioritizing
- Having a tendency to fantasize
- Not being able to sit still for even brief periods
- Acting impulsively
- Craving exciting—and even dangerous— activities
- Interrupting conversations often with irrelevant comments

The attention deficit brain storm, a brain stress pattern, is very difficult to diagnose based upon behavior alone. Professional clinicians must administer tests to properly diagnose this condition because a multitude of other disorders have the same (or nearly the same) symptoms involving attention and concentration. For example, any one of the disorders listed below can negatively impact attention and concentration capabilities:

- Grief

- Anxiety

- Depression

- Being in love

- Poor sleep

- Fatigue

- Post-traumatic stress

- Psychosis

Interventions for addicted risk-taking or ADHD teenagers

The key with these teenagers is to find ways to stimulate their brains without resorting to drugs that can lead to dependency and addiction. Methods for doing so include:

- Encourage engagement with music. The rhythms of music appear to excite the brain of ADHD-prone teenagers in helpful ways. Teaching ADHD-diagnosed teenagers to play a musical instrument or getting them involved in singing and dancing may prove highly beneficial in curbing anxiety and high-risk behavior.

- Suggest controlled-breathing exercises that can help the brain "turn on." This does not involve fast breathing that can cause hyperventilation. The best techniques involve breathing at a rate of six to eight breaths per minute. One helpful device is the emWave, produced by HeartMath (www.heartmathstore.com). This tool trains the user in calming their breathing while providing heart rhythm feedback. This allows the user to quickly see how the breathing techniques slow heart rate and reduce anxiety.

- Promote chewing gum, which can help stimulate the brain and lower anxiety.

- Employ the BAUD (BioAcoustical Utilization Device). At the Origins Recovery Centers, we use this sound machine, which produces frequencies similar to brain waves. (A more detailed description of how the device works is in Chapter 7.) The machine stimulates the brain's natural healing ability in order to balance neural activity. We have found that ADHD teenagers using this device consistently improve their performance in school and just seem happier in general. The goal is to use the sound waves the machine produces to alter the child's brain patterns and achieve a desired state of mind, such as joy, peace, comfort, and other antianxiety states. Since there are no negative side effects, the machine can be used whenever the child wants to feel better. Some ADHD patients use it to aid concentration while studying. In our clinic, we also use EEG recordings to monitor brain patterns to help reinforce patients' newfound abilities and to help them understand how to manage their emotions.

Self-Critical Teenagers

Kelly was a bright but self-critical girl, anxious about her performance as a student and, particularly, as a dancer. The hypercompetitive environment of New York City, where Kelly lived and trained, eventually overwhelmed her, and she became depressed. She lost weight and was often sick.

Her stress levels rose dramatically after Kelly broke her arm in the finals at a national competition. She felt she had disappointed her parents and wasted years of preparation. As she sank deeper into her depression, Kelly began using drugs to self-medicate. She quickly became addicted and dropped out of high school and ended her once-promising career as a dancer. Within two years, she was working as a prostitute to finance a heroin habit.

Kelly is among those young people who lack coping skills to deal with self-inflicted pressures. Many overly self-critical teenagers become alcoholics, drug abusers, or other types of addicts. The type A teenager has a narrow definition of success, but the self-critical teenager has few defined goals. The self-critical teenager doesn't see success as an option. The message in this teenager's head is: *I'm bad.*

Characteristics of self-critical teenagers

- Being anxious and depressed
- Having low energy
- Having difficulty dealing with failure
- Suddenly losing interest in once-favorite activities
- Being devoid of joy and laughter
- Refusing to discuss personal problems or concerns

Interventions for addicted self-critical teenagers

Teenagers who are severely self-critical often require professional therapy—although these suggestions may help in the meantime:

- Encourage your teenager to listen to and play music, drum, sing, dance, and get physical exercise.
- Give your teenager subtle praise for things he or she does well, but beware of going overboard with compliments, as this will most likely backfire.
- Encourage your teenager to do volunteer work or otherwise get involved with projects helping others in order to shift

the focus off of him- or herself and any
perceived problems.

- Make sure you are not modeling self-critical
  behavior yourself.

Teenagers with Poor Problem-Solving Skills

Joseph was a gentle and good-humored soul with
many friends. He thrived in groups, and had many
strong leadership skills—but he had poor problem-
solving skills and a serious aversion to conflict. Joseph's
parents had a troubled relationship, and conflict was a
constant in his home. Alcohol was usually a factor in
parental battles. His parents either shunned each other
in silence or lashed out violently, hurting each other and
damaging the home environment.

Joseph had no exposure to compromise or peaceful
conflict resolution. As the fourth of seven children, he
received very little parental nurturing. He learned to
lie low, avoiding attention and ducking conflict. This
behavior carried over into his school and social relationships. Joseph was generally quiet and agreeable. He
preferred not to be noticed, so his teachers and counselors had difficulty knowing what was going on with him.

In his early teens, Joseph had many acquaintances
drawn by his agreeable nature, but he shied away from
close friendships. Emotionally wounded because of his
warring and inattentive parents, the boy self-medicated
with alcohol—and he usually drank alone. When he
did so, a darker side emerged; and Joseph, mirroring his
parents, sometimes turned violent. The usually docile
teen lashed out when under the influence, and unwary

victims, taken by surprise, were injured as a result. One discussion with a fellow student over the basketball prowess of different racial groups led to a particularly violent outburst in which Joseph nearly killed the other boy.

By the age of 22, Joseph was a serious alcoholic. He'd burned through two marriages and three unsuccessful trips to rehab. Counselors often described him as the "nicest guy in the program," but within six months of completion, he would always be drinking again and fighting with another girlfriend.

Characteristics of teenagers with poor problem-solving skills

- Avoiding conflicts and disagreements
- Preferring to "tag along," rarely forming strong bonds with peers
- Never expressing strong opinions about anything
- Responding to conflict by isolating themselves
- Displaying poor self-esteem and little interest in self-analysis

Interventions for addicted teenagers with poor problem-solving skills

If your teenager falls into this category, he or she needs to learn to resolve conflicts and work on ways to solve problems without retreating into isolation or giving up. This isn't an easy process, of course, but here are a few ways teens can be encouraged to learn these skills:

- Teach them to assess each viewpoint without emotional attachments or the need to be right.

- Encourage them to understand different viewpoints.

- Suggest findIng a commuon ground when they are in a conflict with someone else (including you) so they can better work toward agreement, even if they just agree to disagree.

- Consider stress management. The emWave mentioned in the section on risk-taking and ADHD teenagers can be helpful for this.

The Teenager with Helicopter Parents

Sophie started out in life as a disadvantaged child. She was not deprived mentally, emotionally, or economically—instead, she was deprived of her autonomy. Her loving and doting mother was so enraptured with her daughter that she barely gave her room to breathe. Sophie was a beautiful child, with an adorable smile and easy manner. She wanted to please her mother, which was good—while it lasted.

By age three, Sophie was performing in beauty pageants. At first, she reveled in the attention and loved to dress up and perform, but the constant hovering of her "helicopter mom" became a major issue. Helicopter parents are those who, for whatever reason, need to dominate or control nearly every moment of a child's life.

In Sophie's case, her mother served not only as parent but pageant coach, agent, and business manager. Her mom was driven by her own failed ambitions for stardom and attention. Mostly, her mother fed her own ego by parading her beautiful child onstage in costly competitions that consumed every waking hour of Sophie's childhood.

The child-beauty-pageant world is particularly rife with helicopter parents, but the same breed thrives in the world of Little League and Pee Wee Football, too. In fact, I quit coaching Little League baseball because it became less about sportsmanship and healthy competition and more about grooming "prospects" for the major leagues.

The saddest aspect of hovering parents is that most do feel that they are simply doing what is best for their children—and their intentions are usually good, if somewhat misguided. For example, helicopter parents demand that their children be placed in advanced programs that they think will guarantee their acceptance into college and their future success. Often, the child's own desires and interests are not a priority.

In most cases, teenagers with hovering parents lack any sense of self-worth because everything is spoon-fed to them, provided for them, and scheduled by their parents, who live through them or make their lives about dominating them. Such teens also need instant gratification because their parents are constantly giving them feedback. These teenagers often don't know what they want, because they've always been told what to do; they have never had a chance to decide for themselves.

Hovering, domineering parents can rob teenagers of their sense of identity and self-determination. These teenagers may never develop self-discipline, good judgment, or their own interests because they grow up dependent on their parents to make their decisions for them. Or, as often happens, they rebel against the parents or use alcohol or drugs to numb themselves.

Characteristics of teenagers with helicopter parents

- Having difficulty making decisions, even about what meal to order or what movie to watch

- Needing instant feedback and gratification, which can be manifested in a preference for activities like playing video games

- Basing their self-esteem on what others say rather than how they feel about themselves

- Being followers—and not leaders—and often trying to fit in with large groups where there is no pressure on them to make decisions

- Lacking a long-term vision, as if waiting for their parents to tell them what they want them to do

- Having difficulty leaving the nest and creating their own lives based on their own interests, with their own circle of friends

<u>Interventions for addicted teenagers with
helicopter parents</u>

Of course, the first intervention for teenagers with helicopter parents is all about the parents and not the teenagers. Such parents must learn to back off and allow their children to develop their own lives. If you think you may be a helicopter parent, or if you have been accused of this by others, consider getting some support in learning to allow your teenager to express his or her own opinions and pursue his or her own dreams. A major goal for teenagers with helicopter parents is to help them become more self-aware, self-confident, and secure in making decisions and creating visions for their lives. Setting goals and working toward them is beneficial for children who have been overprotected and under constant guidance. The following techniques are often helpful:

- Encourage your teenager to share his or her opinions as often as possible. Give fewer instructions and ask more questions—and seem genuinely interested in the answers.

- Promote participation in charitable organizations. Focusing on others is an excellent way to gain a fresh perspective on life and its blessings. There are many rewards to be reaped by a teenager who dedicates some time and effort to a cause greater than his or her own. Habitat for Humanity is one a volunteer organization that's popular among teenagers, although other philanthropic and service organizations also exist in every community.

- Encourage travel as way to adjust perspective. Suggest spiritually themed trips, such as a visit to the Holy Land or to mystical and beautiful areas such as Stonehenge in England, the Sanctuary of Apollo in Greece, Machu Picchu in Peru, or the Grand Canyon and Sedona in Arizona.

Intervention Methods for Every Child

Any child can fall victim to drug and alcohol abuse and addiction. There is no safe "type" of child who is immune to the lure of drugs, and there is no inoculation to assure that your teenager will never fall into this dangerous pit. Parents must walk a fine line between good parenting and being overprotective.

I recommend educating your children about the dangers of addiction at an early age, long before they have access to either alcohol or drugs. Age six is a good time to begin a preventive program. Don't overdo it to the point that you raise your child's curiosity, but instead approach the hazards of drug and alcohol in the same way you warn about fire, lightning, and traffic. Be straight with your child, even if you've abused drugs or alcohol in the past. You can serve as a good example, and as a good example of a bad example. As the child gets older and more aware of the world, you can be more frank and more graphic in describing dangers.

Stoic parents who tend not to encourage open discussions need to be aware that it is critically important to establish open lines of communication with children early and often. Be mindful that it doesn't matter what is being said so much as that the conversations are candid and ongoing. Most of the time, what is said won't matter all that much—but there may come a time when having those open lines of communication may save your child's life.

Your child may want to talk about the latest pop star, hairstyles, soccer players, or video games. Those topics may not appeal to you, but remember, it's not the subject matter that is important. If you can talk about things that don't matter now, then you should be able to talk about things that really do matter later on. Insist upon honest expression of feelings, and be sure to practice the art of listening. Fathers in particular want to be problem solvers—but sometimes your child just wants you to listen, understand, and empathize.

Don't be afraid to inquire as to whether your child's friends are using drugs or alcohol. Explain that you aren't there to judge them or to turn them in; instead, you need to be comfortable about your child hanging out with them. But if you learn of other children who are using drugs and alcohol, you do have a responsibility to alert those who care about them and can steer them away from abuse and addiction. This is an invasion of your community. Stand ready to join the fight.

✦ ✦ ✦

PART II

ADDICTION AND ACTION PLANS FOR THE TEENAGE BRAIN

CHAPTER THREE

THE DANGERS OF HIGH-RISK BEHAVIOR IN THE STILL-DEVELOPING BRAIN

Addiction is a disease centered primarily in the brain. It is not a virus or bacteria, but rather a chronic biological condition that eventually eliminates all reasoning and creates a total breakdown of behavior controlled by values. Addiction will, unless checked, result in death.

There is some controversy over whether addiction should be defined as a "habit" rather than a disease. The general criterion used to determine if an addiction is a disease is whether a person has control of the outcome, along with whether his or her life is being negatively affected by the use of drugs and alcohol. A true addict cannot stop abusing drugs and alcohol—even to save his or her life. Some compare true drug and alcohol addiction to the case of a type 2 diabetic, whose metabolism has been modified to the point that there is no controlling what the body needs.

There also is a boundary between habit and disease based on brain toxicity and behavior. Addiction begins as a habit—and any habit has the potential to become a disease. Indeed, some people have an inherited predisposition to addiction. Many times psychological factors play a huge part. Addictions often take root when someone tries to self-medicate because of anxieties, and then dependency is seeded. The younger a person is when an addiction takes hold, the more difficult it is to break the cycle of addiction.

How Does Addiction Happen?

Consider the two small almond-shaped parts of the brain, about three inches behind the eyes, called *nucleus accumbens*. As briefly touched on earlier, these areas are known to regulate pleasure. Our bodies generate a chemical called *dopamine* that functions as a neurotransmitter, sending pleasure signals to the brain. Most of us can receive the dopamine and other natural stimulants in our systems and convert them into joyful life experiences. In the 1950s, brain researchers James Olds and Peter Milner implanted electrodes into the nucleus accumbens of a rat's brain and found that the rat chose to press a lever that stimulated it. The rat preferred pressing the lever to receive pleasure over choosing to eat or drink.

The nucleus accumbens have been studied for their role in addiction, but they play an equal role in processing pleasure sensations, such as those triggered by food and sex. Interestingly, the nucleus accumbens are activated by music, sugar-based food, sexual sensations, and certain drugs. For example, cocaine creates a rate of arousal 100 times that triggered by food. Sex creates about 300 times the rate of arousal triggered by food.

For some, especially those diagnosed with ADHD, the nucleus accumbens have been found to be only 50

percent as efficient as the average person in metaboliz-
ing dopamine. Many addicts will say that using stimulants makes them feel "normal" and as happy as "normal
people." One could reasonably see why there could be a
DNA link to addiction of this nature.

The Slippery Slope

When a person habitually uses drugs or alcohol, the
brain adjusts and requires more of the substance in order
to release its natural stimulants. The brain is focused
on what Freud called the "pleasure principle," and the
function that brings us the most pleasure will get our
attention.

Think of the neurons that connect different spots in
the brain like telephone circuits that only carry happy
conversations. Since we have more than 200 billion of
these neuron connections, they can quickly govern our
brains. Neurons crave connections. When a neuron is
not used, it reconnects to something that will use it—
and the most attractive bidder for that connection is a
pleasure arousal center. What happens is that big holes
start to appear in the brain, which limits its thinking
capacity, especially in what motivates it. The holes are
due to the toxicity caused by the abused substances. The
brain starts cutting off all circuits except those that pertain to the pleasure routes. (Indeed, in an addict's brain
there is so little activity going on in some areas related
to long-range thinking and good judgment that those
areas appear "blank" in brain scans.)

As a neuropsychologist, I find it fascinating that the
nucleus accumbens is so closely tied to the forebrain so

that rewiring for gratification occurs so rapidly. The fore-brain lobe is where thoughts are organized and actions are triggered to assure our survival and our pleasure. The forebrain lobe is also the part of the brain where dysfunctions in concentration, such as attention deficit disorder, can be mapped.

A noted study once found that addicts tend to see words associated with drugs more quickly than other words, which led scientists to believe that addiction is centered in the brain, where it becomes hardwired and triggers rapid responses. I mention this study as confirmation that the addicted brain globally focuses on drugs. The disease takes over the brain to the point that it reacts immediately to any stimulation associated with drugs. This is similar to the state of mind of a starving person who craves food so much that every thought is directed at obtaining it.

When a brain rewires to focus on the pleasures derived from addictive drugs, the consequences include:

- Taking involuntary actions to gain more drugs, meaning that the addict has no remorse for any consequences of this overriding drive

- The need for drugs overruling rational judgment

- Buildup of toxicity in the body, which will impair and create disease in the liver and other elimination organs (including the kidneys, lungs, and digestive tract)

- Blockages of channels for other medications and drugs, which result in confusing side

effects and even reversals of expected
results, making treatment of emotional and
mental symptoms problematic

Teenage Brain Pruning

As if drug damage and brain chaos are not enough,
teenagers are vulnerable because the brain essentially rewires itself during adolescence. A cascade of hormones
floods the teenage brain, stimulating a major overhaul.
If you picture the brain as a tree, the teenage sapling
suddenly begins spreading its branches. In the brain,
this is the expansion of neuron contacts that allows for
learning and survival.

In addition, a "pruning" of the brain begins at about
14 years of age for girls and 16 years of age for boys (although this varies by culture and nutritional quality).
Returning to the metaphor of the tree, some weaker
branches are eliminated in favor of stronger ones. As a
result, a teenager begins to mature with more distinctive
mental and physical skill sets. At the same time, some
cognitive abilities recede.

This pruning also has tremendous impact on a teenager's ability to make judgments. For approximately two
to three years, lasting up to nine years, there is a major
reduction of reasoning in two areas: future ramifications
of present behavior and empathy. Teenagers often lose
the ability to understand the consequences of their behaviors. (For example, taking nude photos and posting
them on the Internet may seem like a fun idea—but
many teenagers experience serious consequences if the
photos are widely circulated in cyberspace.)

The loss of empathy in adolescents whose brains are rewiring results in self-absorption and self-centeredness —to the point that a teenager often has no capacity for understanding a parent's concern for missed curfews or poor grades. Teenagers challenge family values and feel as though rules do not necessarily apply to them.

Protecting the Vulnerable Child

Lack of judgment and self-absorption can cause a teenager to experiment with drugs and alcohol and engage in irresponsible sexual behavior. There is little you as a parent can do to prevent the developmental issues caused by brain changes in adolescents—but you can work to protect your teenager from potential disaster by following these three suggestions:

1. Plan ahead. Take time to talk to your kids about the changes in the brain that occur during adolescence. This is not about making threats. It's more about aiding self-understanding and planning for potential conflicts and confusion. Be clear that sometimes bad things just happen, and prepare your child by offering assurance that you will love him or her no matter what occurs and that you will always be there in times of need. Discuss potential problems and how you might work through them as a family. Be sure to be clear, too, about responsibilities and consequences. One key to making sure your teenager doesn't tune you out is to use a caring and non-threatening tone.

2. Educate. Teens usually hate "educational" talks, so it's best to keep them brief, but do cover topics such as the importance of maintaining trust, moral values, being conscious of physical safety, and the dangers of drug and alcohol abuse in some depth. If you feel unqualified to discuss any of these topics, ask for help from a professional counselor at school, in your church, in a social-services agency, or in private practice.

3. Offer stories that feature role models. As your child enters adolescence, present books, articles, and movies about exemplary individuals. Teenagers need positive role models, and they often readily identify with underdogs who have overcome challenges. Of course, parents can be positive role models themselves, but don't hesitate to expose your teenager to additional examples. Otherwise, teens sometimes find and emulate their own negative role models—including those who might use drugs, abuse alcohol, or indulge in other self-destructive behaviors.

✦ ✦ ✦

CHAPTER FOUR

BRAIN PLASTICITY AND ITS ROLE IN ADDICTION TREATMENT

A stroke victim who cannot speak due to a brain injury can learn to use another part of the brain to reacquire the power of speech. I've known patients who were crippled in auto accidents but taught their brains new ways to move their legs so they could walk again. The same brain-retraining processes can work for brains damaged by addiction and the toxic effects of drugs. Our latest successes in rewiring and rehabilitating the brain are due to new technology and a greater understanding of brain plasticity. There are three basic principles for using brain plasticity to deal with the damage done by addiction.

BRAIN PLASTICITY PRINCIPLE I:
Neurons That Learn Together Reinforce Each Other

Here's a catchy little brain refrain for you: *Neurons that fire together, wire together.* The more neural conduits share common frequency patterns, the more the neurons can combine into common activities, such as thinking patterns. This is the basis for habit formation—both good and bad.

In neurological terms, we call similarities in frequency waveforms "coherence" patterns. Neurological pathways form networks when they merge, and this helps to build and refine efficient brain pathways. This process continues as long as it is appropriately reinforced.

Coaching Principles

After I graduated from college, my dream was to become a great coach. My first job was coaching middle-school football, basketball, and track. I wasn't a very good football coach, but I did have success in basketball and track. I used my psychological training to alter the brain patterns of my athletes to enhance their performances. My methods were not unique. Many coaches use similar programs when developing fundamental skills. My system was based on the three steps of brain pattern development:

1. Demonstrate and create a visual image of the desired skill.

2. Practice, practice, practice.

3. Celebrate success with positive feedback.

[Repeat.]

Visualization techniques used in athletic coaching can also work to help with addiction. I've had alcoholics imagine situations where they were apt to abuse alcohol, such as when they were frustrated, engulfed in interpersonal conflicts, or feeling blue while in a period of low self-esteem. I had my patients imagine taking constructive steps that would help them deal with these situations without relying on alcohol. I asked them to imagine at least three positive scenarios.

Next, my patients talked about their imagined scenarios with group members. The group's responsibility was to ensure that no details—no matter how small—were ignored. For example, if a person imagined calling a friend or sponsor, someone in the group would ask what the sponsor's name was, whose phone the person used to make the call, what type of phone it was, what was said, what the response might have been, and so on. The patient would continue to recount his or her imagined scenario until all details were rehearsed with complete clarity.

At the conclusion of each group session, each member would have compiled three options in response to potential problems and have committed those plans to memory. This approach was a success with more than 90 percent of the participants in the recovery process (meaning that many followed the "plan" when presented with the real-life scenarios). If someone you care about has a substance-abuse problem, this technique may help.

Remember the three basic steps: *visualization, practice,* and *reward.* You might consider asking an addicted teenager to visualize overcoming the desire to do drugs by playing his favorite sport. We find that even a defiant child may take up the challenge of competition and want to win. Depending on how entrenched the addiction is, a teenager may be willing to visualize using exercise as a replacement for drugs, replaying the image of exercise—and actually engaging in exercise—several times a day. You can also encourage your teenager to reward him- or herself after each occasion that the teen either visualizes or actually plays the sport.

BRAIN PLASTICITY PRINCIPLE II:
Neuron Bundles Are Changed by Experience and Need

It is exceedingly difficult to break a habit simply by announcing the intent to do so. For example, smokers can attest to the challenge of breaking the nicotine habit. We have all experienced the sensation of a "racing" mind in which we can't quiet our thoughts or "shut off" our brains; this is an example of how difficult it can be to disrupt neurological patterns. Among the most difficult neurological patterns to control are the insistent thoughts that come with addiction. Brain activity responsible for addiction *can* be modified by creating new neural pathways. But quite frankly, addicts don't often retrain their brains because they *want* to. They are more likely to do this when they are put into situations where they *need* to.

Over the years, psychiatrists have used a number of disruptive techniques, such as electroshock therapy and the now-outlawed practice of insulin-induced comas, to alter behavior patterns. In Egypt and Ireland, "purposeful rituals," such as nearly drowning someone in hopes that the person would be changed for the better, have been used to alter undesirable behaviors.

Techniques for Success—Changing Patterns

Professionals offer a number of these seemingly extreme methods to help addicted teenagers. One method is to disrupt brain activity through altered states of consciousness. Such states can be reached through a variety of techniques, such as:

- Sensory deprivation (solitary experiences, such as vision quests, confinement, and sensory-deprivation chambers)

- Overstimulation (for example, hyperventilation, a firewalker's trance, and shamanistic trances)

- Profound relaxation (including hypnosis, mystical inductions, and sonic rhythms)

The way this works is similar to how stroke victims can learn to use different parts of their brains to relearn abilities they have lost. Changing addictive mind-sets can work along the same lines. Many people whose brains have suffered trauma and damage have regained function by tapping other parts of the brain.

For example, you can teach a teenager's brain to seek pleasure in other ways besides his or her drug of choice. When a brain detoxes, neurons crave addictive resources. If pleasure centers are stimulated with alternative resources, such as music or rhythmic frequencies (even if they are less stimulating than the drug), the neurons can be trained to accept the alternatives to satisfy the drug and alcohol craving.

Brain Plasticity Principle III:
Brain Growth Can Affect the Ability to Learn

Learning in the brain is not a continuous process. Learning starts and stops rather abruptly with the biochemical dispersion of brain-growth factors. When the brain is growing, the nucleus basalis switches on and coats each neuron with a rich, fatty substance that helps speed up the learning process. The speeded-up learning process, however, doesn't last forever. Eventually, as we age, the brain's learning abilities slow.

Many foods are thought to assist in learning. I have found certain "brain foods" can have an impact, including better focus and control, or even stimulate actual brain growth. High protein (from sources such as eggs and meat), omega-3 and omega-6 (from fish and fish oil), and some complex carbohydrates can aid healing at a cellular level because these nutrients are the building blocks for cell growth and repair. These will be discussed more fully in Chapter 5.

Sometimes, the brain slows down abruptly due to lack of attention and positive reinforcement. To learn, you must intentionally focus the brain. You also have to be excited about what you are doing. The emotional edge helps open up the door to learning.

Intention and Attention:
New Pathways Can Be Altered and Reset

Working with addicts can be frustrating, especially when you believe the addict is making progress but then he or she backslides by making bad decisions and behaving in self-destructive ways. Imagine clearing your garden only to have weeds reappear a few days later! The challenge in working with addicts is to keep making steady and stable progress. So . . . how do you do that?

Practice. It takes practice and time for an addict's brain to reorganize itself. New learned behaviors can't help the addict if the behaviors don't become ingrained. A famous golfer was asked what it was like to play a game for a living. He replied, "You see me on the course, swinging my club maybe 70 times. What you didn't see was me practicing each shot over 100,000 times during years and years of training." Michael Jordan became one of the greatest basketball players of all time by practicing shots hour upon hour over many years. Potential means nothing without persistent practice and skill development.

The brain's plasticity gives every addict the power to change addictive behaviors by reorganizing neural networks. But you have to follow a plan and practice new behaviors to tap that power. This process of creating new connections in the brain even has a cool name—*neurogenesis*—which refers to the birthing of nerve cells and represents the front line of the healing process.

The key to being able to fully integrating these neural-pathway changes is to experience joy and happiness in the process—a vital step that is often missed. That means that in order to *change* the brain, an addicted teenager needs to make the brain happier by exercising it (mastering tasks he or she wants to master) and celebrating his or her victories and successes. Unless the brain gets positive reinforcement, it won't create new pathways.

An addicted teenager might say that he used drugs because there wasn't anything better to do, or because he was bored or lonely. If you ask a drug-free teenager why he doesn't go along with the crowd and use drugs, the response is usually, "I have better things to do with my life." What the sober teenager means is that he is getting a better payoff from other activities than he could expect to get from drugs.

✦ ✦ ✦

CHAPTER FIVE

HEALING THE BRAINS OF TEENAGE ADDICTS

A brain damaged by drugs and alcohol is not easily restored to health. Detoxification can take a year or more, depending on the level of abuse. I recommend several natural approaches to cleansing and healing the brain, including nutritional supplements, breathing techniques, and music therapy, each of which I will discuss in this chapter.

However, before you begin these approaches, I highly recommend an assessment to determine the damage caused to the brain by the abuse. These tests can be performed by a licensed neuropsychologist, but you as a parent can perform some basic evaluations to better gauge the issues. Such a parental assessment can provide a base to use for comparison as your teenager undergoes professional treatment.

The major brain functions to assess include:

- Moods
- Judgment
- Reliability
- Memory

- Value systems
- Disruption of thought processes
- Lack of overall functioning

The last three are very difficult for nonprofessionals to measure, but the first four are easier to assess. In Chapter 2, we already discussed mood changes to look for in the early detection of addictive behaviors, and here I'll present information on assessing judgment, reliability, and memory as well. When making assessments, keep in mind that age, too, is a factor. A teenager's level of mature judgment and cognitive skills is dependent on the intensity of the drug usage, which can be affected by the age at which drug or alcohol abuse began. For example, if a child begins abusing drugs at the age of 10, even if he is sober by the age of 30, his emotional age may hover closer to 10.

Assessing Judgment

Judgment is difficult to assess with any predictability, but you can determine your child's judgment abilities to some extent by assessing answers to a few questions about fantasy scenarios. Here are some examples:

Judgment Scenario #1:

A husband and wife are fighting over which dress their daughter will be allowed to wear to a dance. They cannot agree on which dress is appropriate. The father insists on a modest pink dress, and the mother insists on a somewhat less modest yellow dress. Suddenly, the father stops fighting and turns to the daughter, making this comment: "It is up to you. Whatever makes you happy." He then leaves. Why did the father leave it up to the daughter?

The correct answer (although there are many other options) relates to the father's wisdom in understanding that the argument was causing stress on the family. He decided that he did not have to "win" the battle. If the teenager taking the assessment believes the father made his decision because "he just got tired of fighting," such an answer may show that the teenager lacks the empathy necessary for making such judgments.

Judgment Scenario #2:

Charlie's friend Ross needs to borrow some money. Ross asks Charlie for $200, which just about breaks Charlie's bank account. Still, Charlie gives his friend the money because Ross promises to repay him within the month. Ross claims he needs the money to help a sick aunt— but Charlie knows this is not true. Ross never returns the money. When Charlie asks for the money back at the end of the month, Ross gets angry and says, "After all, what are good friends for?" Ross was wrong. But *why* was Ross wrong?

A healthy teenager's response will focus on the importance of trust in relationships. If the answer does not refer to trust, then the teenager's judgment lacks insight and the ability to take a long-term view.

Judgment Scenario #3:

Sixteen-year-old Marty wants to go to a concert, but his father and mother are worried that he might drink and hurt himself and others. Marty lies to his parents, saying he will be accompanied by his trusted friend Joe. Instead, Marty picks up three less reliable buddies, who convince Marty to skip the concert and hit the bars instead. That night, Marty wrecks his car but is unhurt. The accident is another driver's fault. Marty's parents are relieved that he was not hurt, but they are also upset that he lied to them about his plans for the night. Marty demands an apology from his parents for not trusting him. Is Marty correct in demanding such an apology?

A healthy response acknowledges that regardless of who is at fault, Marty did lie to his parents, and he needs to be accountable for his deception. If your teenager doesn't see that Marty should be held accountable, then this indicates they lack the understanding and insight necessary for making correct decisions.

Assessing Reliability

Does your teenager fulfill promises and agreements? For example, if your teenager agrees to take out the trash, wash the car, and take the dog for a walk once a day but rarely follows through, he or she receives a low reliability grade. If your child completes tasks most of the time, rate him or her "moderate." A "good" rating goes to those who take responsibility for tasks every time. Anything less than a good rating may be due to poor memory or disorganization—which might suggest a neurological problem.

Assessing Memory

Testing verbal or numerical concepts is helpful in assessing memory. For example, you can test a teenager's ability to recall information by reciting a list of numbers and asking the teenager to repeat the list in the same order. The average teenager should correctly repeat at least five digits in a row. If you prefer to test your child's memory in a way that doesn't rely on numbers, use a story. For example:

> Kelly was a poor but ambitious 17-year-old girl. She had a bakery job making cookies and doughnuts, for which she was paid $10 an hour. She bought her own clothes and rented a room behind a hotel. She got her breakfasts for free at the doughnut shop, and she cleaned the hotel's kitchen in exchange for dinner every night. She was very proud of herself and happy with her life.

Ask your teenager to remember as many details as possible from the story, such as Kelly's name and her jobs. The average teenager should remember about seven details from the story. If your teen cannot, he or she is distracted or has memory distortion, lacks motivation, or may be too anxious to remember.

If a teenager's brain takes longer to process information, he or she may be quick to give up on communication with a parent if the parent is talking too fast or too loudly. An addict's brain often runs in slow motion, and concepts may be too complex for a given discussion. In speaking to a teenager with poor concentration levels, a parent must ask questions that are simply stated and easily grasped. Sometimes an addicted teenager can only understand one-step or two-step instructions.

Once you've made a baseline assessment, you can begin supporting your teenager's addiction treatment with several natural approaches that I have found very helpful.

Nurturing Your Child's Brain: Vitamins and Supplements

Three different vitamins and supplements are particularly useful in healing an addict's brain: omega-3 fatty acids, thiamine (vitamin B_1), and vitamin D. Let's take a look at each of these.

Omega-3 fatty acids. Research shows that the brain benefits from omega-3 fats, the "brain food" stars. Omega-3 fats are used for neuron insulation, which increases the speed of nerve impulses and connections. Omega-3 fats are also known to combat depression, enhance learning and memory, and aid in brain plasticity and creating new neural pathways needed for constructive changes in the brain.

Omega-3 oils come in several types and are contained in substances that don't require prescriptions. In food, omega-3 fats come in three varieties: *alpha-Linolenic acid* (ALA), *eicosapentaenoic acid* (EPA), and *docosahexaenoic acid* (DHA). ALA is found mostly in plant foods such as flax, soybeans, and vegetables. These substances are converted into EPA and DHA in the body. EPA and DHA are also found in fish. Just a four-ounce portion of salmon twice a week provides about five grams of omega-3s, an excellent weekly supplement.

Thiamine (vitamin B$_1$). This substance helps manufacture *acetylcholine,* one of the brain's major messengers, or neurotransmitters. Acetylcholine triggers the metabolic process that helps the brain better process food. The best place to find vitamin B$_1$ is in nuts and grains.

Vitamin D. This is also known as the "sunshine" vitamin because it comes from exposure to the sun. It is vital to the brain and may be a factor in fending off Alzheimer's. Vitamin D is critical for maintaining the ratio of calcium and phosphorus in the body, as well as for promoting the growth of nerve cells. Vitamin D is helpful in repairing injured brains, particularly in the *hippocampus,* the primary memory control center.

Strategic Nutritional Plan for Memory Enhancement

Memory loss is associated with many types of brain injuries, including those caused by drug or alcohol abuse. Memory, critical for learning and storing new information, is most often tested when measuring general intelligence. A number of supplements can aid memory. They include:

Acetyl-L-Carnitine (up to 1,000 mg per day), which promotes the activity of two neurotransmitters—*acetylcholine* and *dopamine*—both of which improve communication within the brain, enhancing creativity, higher-level problem solving, reflex speed, and efficiency.

Alpha Glyceryl Phosphoryl Choline (Alpha-GPC) (400 mg three times per day), which is rich in *choline* (a major ingredient in chicken eggs), a substance shown to raise IQ scores (you can take this as an individual supplement as well—see below). Alpha-GPC combines glycerol and phosphate, which together protect brain-cell membranes that improve memory function. Alpha-GPC appears to help restore some function in stroke patients and may well be beneficial in treating other brain injuries.

Choline (1,500 mg per day), which is widely applauded as a mental stimulant that makes you smarter. It is produced within your body from two amino acids, *methionine* and *serine*, with help from vitamin B_{12} and folic acid.

Ginseng (200–400 mg per day), which is probably the herb that gets the most press for promoting good health and mental alertness. Ginseng is beneficial because it contains *ginsenosides,* which stimulate neurotransmitters so that the brain can synthesize proteins for fuel.

Rhodiola (100–400 mg per day), which is a Siberiangrown herb that soldiers have used for stamina and which is also useful for treating depression.

The Cleansing Breath

Breathing is necessary for survival, of course, but it also serves about 2,000 other specific functions for the body, including cleansing it of toxins. When you inhale, you take in nitrogen and oxygen (which have many benefits for the body and mind). Exhaling helps release toxic carbon dioxide and other gases.

Teaching addicted or drug-using teenagers breath control can give them another tool to help deal with cravings and impulses. Proper breathing techniques can also reduce stress. When we are stressed or frightened, for example, we often engage in stressful quick and rapid breathing.

I've noticed students who hardly breathe at all while taking tests because they are so stressed, but this is counterproductive, because you need to breathe easily to perform at high levels. In my own student days, I decided for some reason that it would help my performance as an athlete if I held my breath while running. I was wrong—and my statistics reflected that error in judgment.

Fortunately, my track coach, Tommy Hinson, took a personal interest in me. He placed me on the cross-country team and gave me a five-mile course to run. "You can walk," he told me, "but you cannot stop—and keep breathing." I thought I would die until I realized that coordinating my breathing with my stride could give me more energy.

In the same way, teenagers can increase energy levels by coordinating breathing with the heartbeat. This is accomplished with the following steps:

- Find your pulse, usually on your wrist or neck, or put your hand on your chest. Begin to count the beats.

- Breathe in and out to the same number of beats. For example, if you inhale for five beats, then breathe out to five beats.

- Take long and comfortable breaths from your belly.

- Practice at least three times a day.

The Six-Step Breath Cleansing Exercise

Here is another breathing exercise that helps clear the brain and lungs and has a number of positive effects, including a possible reduction in flu and colds. This exercise usually takes about five minutes.

1. Put your right hand over your belly button and your left hand over your heart. Begin to breathe so that your right hand is moving as you do so but your left hand is not. (This is related to diaphragmatic or belly breathing.) Continue for at least 20 breaths.

2. With your hands in the same position, breathe in such a way that your left hand is moving but your right one is not. (This is often called *chest breathing*.) Do this for 20 breaths.

3. Breathe in and out by raising and lowering your shoulders. Do not let either hand move. Do this for ten breaths.

4. Move your hands and your shoulders and breathe in and out five times.

5. As you inhale, hold your breath for the count of three, then exhale in spurts, as if you are coughing. Exhale all the way. This helps rid the lungs of toxins. (If you're a smoker, you may see smoke even if you haven't had a cigarette for several days!)

6. Return to your normal breathing pattern.

Do this at least twice a day.

Music for Brain Health and as a Treatment for Addiction

Research shows that music can be soothing for addicts. Our positive response to the rhythms in music can be traced to the womb, where our mothers' heartbeat is one of the first sounds we hear. The heart, the central organ of the body, beats at a rhythmic pace that affects our moods and level of motivation.

Many of my patients who have been addicted to powerful drugs have discovered rhythmic exercises can be a much safer and saner alternative. I've witnessed the power of music and rhythmic therapies firsthand and have seen their far-reaching effects. One example is the Stomp for Life program, sponsored by the University of North Texas Medical School, which Dr. Susan Franks and I developed as part of a weight-management program. It consisted of three songs with accompanying dance routines for fifth and sixth graders. The lyrics were about the importance of eating right.

The results were amazing. Heavy children lost weight and sedentary children were more active—but we were also surprised to discover that symptoms of type 2 diabetes were reversed for some children. Most of all, the kids loved performing the songs and dance routines. Parents reported that their children started requesting the healthier foods promoted in the songs.

Parents of addicted or at-risk children could use similar music programs to help ease cravings. At the very least, parents can encourage teenagers to listen to soothing music, using it as a means to bond with their teenagers. Consider the campfire drum and dancing rituals in tribal cultures. In those gatherings, members of the group bond. The same can happen around stereo speakers in a modern living room. Drumbeats, music, and serene lighting can have a positive impact on troubled teenagers and their concerned parents.

✦ ✦ ✦

PART III

WHAT PARENTS AND FAMILY CAN DO TO TREAT THE TEENAGE ADDICT

CHAPTER SIX

TREATING YOUR ADDICTED TEENAGER'S DEPRESSION

Lois walked into my clinic with half-closed eyelids. I know the look well: the teenager was stoned. Through further investigation, I learned that Lois had snorted cocaine sometime within the last 24 hours. Her parents were incensed that their daughter was taking drugs— and they and wanted her treated quickly and quietly.

For six years, Lois had been an honor student in a private school, but she lost focus when she moved to a public school. Both her motivation and her grades dropped. She was tutored during summer, but she was still failing her eighth-grade courses.

In my sessions with her, Lois revealed that she hit a major stumbling block that first year in public school. As the oldest of three sisters, she felt pressured by her parents to serve as a good example. Keeping her grades up became an obsession. Public school was a shock for her because of the lack of discipline and the many classroom distractions. She had never encountered so many young people from different cultural and economic backgrounds. She felt threatened and unsure of herself.

At first, Lois responded to her insecurities by studying harder. She increased her study time from two hours a day to six or seven hours, often falling asleep with her books in hand. Her family considered these intense hours to be positive confirmation that Lois was taking her schoolwork seriously, and they praised her. As Lois continued to study with even greater intensity, she soon began drinking coffee to help her stay awake so she could keep reading. Soon, she was sleeping only four hours each night. Despite her efforts, she was getting only B's and C's. Lois continued to push herself—and she ignored her body's need for rest.

Lois was so focused on pleasing her parents with good grades that she had no friends. Her unhappiness grew when the one thing she had dedicated herself to—raising her grades—did not happen. She became withdrawn and gave up on her studies. Lois eventually fell in with a group at school characterized by family turmoil, disaffection, insecurities, and loneliness. When the group introduced her to marijuana and cocaine, Lois believed she had found her first friends in this new school.

After a few months of drug use, Lois wanted to do little else. Once she was drawn into their circle, her new friends stopped giving her drugs and began demanding payment. They wanted money, which Lois stole from her mother's purse. When she didn't have money to exchange for drugs, they asked for sex—and she agreed. Lois's drug use went on for about a year. Finally, she was caught at school with crack cocaine. Her parents managed to get her placed in outpatient drug-addiction treatment as an alternative to jail.

To her credit, Lois broke free of her addictions and was anxious to earn her family's forgiveness. She promised to stay away from her druggie friends, and she lived up to that pledge. Her parents put her back in private school, hoping the change of environment would keep her from sliding backward.

Unfortunately, Lois continued to earn poor grades. She grew increasingly depressed—and this state left her at risk for a return to drug addiction. Fortunately, we were able to help Lois. She learned to trust her own judgment and instincts once she was drug-free. She also learned to forgive and love herself so that she was free to forgive and love others as well.

Lois's case is not uncommon. Consider that her primary goal had been to please her parents through good grades. Remember, neurons that fire together, wire together. In Lois's case, her neurons clustered around this one connection (pleasing her parents through schoolwork) to the nucleus accumbens (the pleasure centers). When her grades dropped initially, the pleasure payoff disappeared, so it's likely the neurons began peeling off the pleasure center of the brain.

Then, when Lois was introduced to drugs, her brain's pleasure center lit up and billions of neurons attached. Although her concentration may have initially improved, it was only to focus on securing and taking drugs. When Lois was caught with crack cocaine and put through a rehab program, she again lost her major source of pleasure. Numbness set in again.

Our treatment efforts eventually succeeded in helping Lois return to a normal life without drugs, but only because she became part of the healing process. Before I share her treatment plan, let's focus on *your* child for a bit.

Depression Evaluation

To determine if someone you love may be experiencing depression, consider some of the primary symptoms described below. Answer each question with "all the time," "most of the time," "sometimes," or "never."

1. Your child reports feeling empty inside and appears to lack emotional highs or lows.

2. Your child no longer enjoys doing the things that used to bring happiness and joy.

3. Your child is irritable but denies feeling depressed.

4. Your child shows a marked decrease in interest in any kind of pleasurable activity.

5. Your child has a significant weight loss and claims to have no appetite—even for favorite foods.

6. Your child's sleep patterns are disrupted.

7. Although your child may work at carrying out tasks, it's obvious that he or she feels no sense of accomplishment or pride.

8. Your child's abilities to concentrate and focus have diminished.

9. There is a noticeable sluggishness in your child's behavior that seems unrelated to true fatigue.

10. Your child has difficulty making decisions.

11. Your child has a negative attitude almost all of the time.

12. Although medications, food, or encouragement may help your child become more active, he or she doesn't engage much emotionally.

13. Your child has an underlying attitude of pessimism.

14. Your child seems to be in mourning for something lost.

15. Your child seems to have no passion for life.

Scoring: If you answered "all the time" or "most of the time" for at least eight statements, it's highly likely that your teenager is experiencing depression. If you answered "all the time" or "most of the time" for three to seven statements, then your teenager is likely shutting down emotionally, and I would advise you to seek immediate professional help for him or her.

Depression can be treated in a variety of ways, including both behavioral and spiritual approaches. By using the principles of treatment related to brain plasticity, your teenager can escape the downward spiral of depression that many addicts experience. Some of these methods may sound either too simple or too complex, but I assure you that I have found success using each of them.

Reversing Negative Thinking

To help your teenager build new and positive neural pathways, you must first help them recognize their negative thinking so they can reset their self-destructive thoughts. One fast technique is to have your teenager sniff a pungent or spicy perfume or essential oil, such as peppermint, clove, or rose every time a negative thought enters his or her mind. This distraction acts as a sensory cue, which your teenager can use as a signal to mentally change direction and think new thoughts. Chanting positive phrases over and over again (I recommend a thousand times a day!) can also help create a positive reflexive response and new neural pathways. Some phrases that can be useful include:

- "Although I have made some bad choices, I can still forgive and love myself."

- "Although I have had problems in dealing with relationships, I know I am enough."

- "Regardless of how I have lived, I know that I am worthy."

- "I can do it."

- "I can be my best friend."

Even changing posture can help those in recovery from addiction to reset their thoughts, since body language seems to have at least some effect on mood. Encourage your teenager to pull back his or her shoulders, knees slightly bent. This will encourage a shift toward joyful thinking. This is the posture for victory! I have observed that it is almost impossible to feel anything less than happy when you hold this posture for 30 seconds. Try it.

Getting Quality Sleep

Sleep is often considered the best medicine for any number of diseases, because it can restore many physical and mental functions. Sleep has at least five different levels at which it processes the energies that the brain needs for restoration. Unfortunately, our ability to get enough sleep has been reduced by all of modern society's distractions and demands. I continue to recommend at least eight hours of sleep for everyone, particularly young people trying to recover from alcohol or drug addiction.

I don't recommend pharmaceutical sleep aids, especially for addicts or those susceptible to addiction. These costly drugs can be dangerous, and very few provide the deep sleep that is necessary for brain healing and recovery from trauma.

I learned one very successful method for inducing deep sleep while I was associated with the pediatric burn unit at the University of Texas Southwestern Medical Center, in Dallas. The basic protocol for treating severe burns is to scrape dead skin off the body twice a day to try to eliminate infection. This is a horribly painful procedure, particularly for children.

We know that listening to a mother's heartbeat helps eliminate stress in babies. Similarly, I have used a tick-tock clock to help new puppies go to sleep on their first night away from their mothers. With this in mind, a group of staff members and I produced a drumming heart-rhythm recording for patients who were having sleep difficulties—including those in recovery from drug abuse. By listening to the CD recording we produced, patients reported falling into a deep, restorative sleep. (You can purchase these recordings through www .MindBodySeries.com. Our most popular are the General Relaxation—part of the Anxiety Relief series—and Sleep series.)

To use these CDs effectively, your teenager should listen to the recordings at least 50 times. As your teenager listens over and over, the brain will begin to memorize and anticipate; this brain awareness is important. After a few weeks or months of regular use, he or she can enter into a trance state the moment the recording begins. This is brain plasticity at work.

Touch and Massage

Healing touch and massage methods can work better than drugs to soothe a drug abuser's mental state. You don't even have to physically touch your teenager if you become skilled at healing touch! You can learn to generate caring energy and love through the palms of your hands, and the sensation of energy (heat) can relax and ease the brain.

Before you begin using these methods on your teenager, be sure to rid yourself of anger and frustration. Your breaths should be long and slow. Stress is contagious and can defeat your efforts to soothe your child.

Starting with the feet, employ a soothing motion without too much friction. You'd be surprised how many children, even rebellious teenagers, find this helpful and relaxing. Use a good massage oil to make it easier and to prevent bruising. Move slowly along the length of the muscle attachments, which is the way energy flows in the body. (To cross these tissues can slow blood flow.)

This helps with relaxation and will win your teenager's trust. Remember to keep moving to other parts of the body so that your child doesn't get bored. Five minutes per body area works well. Include the feet, legs, lower back, upper back and shoulders, neck, and scalp.

Some natural-healing philosophies hold that disease is the result of a blockage of healing energies due to trauma or stress. As you move your hands over the muscles of the body, you may encounter one of these blockages in the form of a muscle spasm. These are common signs of stress.

A general landscape of the body and associated stresses is provided below:

Stress association	Area of body
Time urgency	Upper legs
Insecurity	Stomach
Guilt, self-criticism	Chest
Anger	Jaws, right-shoulder trapezius
Overresponsibility, expectancy	Trapezius muscle and low back
Oversensitivity to criticism	Left-shoulder trapezius
Difficulty with acceptance	Neck

Put pressure on the muscle if you find these blockages, and ask your teenager to "breathe out the pain." By pressing on the muscle spasms, you can "milk" the blood through the spasm, releasing muscle tightness. Do not spend too much time on the spasm, however, as too much pressure can also release inflammatory chemicals that make the muscle sore and upset the stomach.

Humming and Toning

Although some people aren't comfortable using their voices as a healing tool, humming or toning can be helpful in relieving stress and healing your child's brain. The vibration of your voice can provide a source for relaxation. Certain notes are associated with specific emotions and parts of the body. By being sensitive to these emotions and associated parts of the body, you can hum or "tone" a teenager into a healing receptivity. Humming with addicted teenagers can lead to major breakthroughs. You might also encourage your child to hum or sing a song that conjures pleasant feelings. Humming and singing to oneself is an ancient healing method and may be the original inspiration for communal singing in church and at celebrations.

The BAUD: Personal Biofeedback Device

The BAUD (BioAccoustical Utilization Device), mentioned previously and described more fully in Chapter 7, is a self-regulation device. It is relatively new to the field, and it is best to consult with a professional on its use. Briefly, the BAUD device sends sonic frequencies into each ear, which serves to calm emotions and combat sadness and despair. The user can control the frequencies and rhythms to create unique and pleasurable sensations. The BAUD is like a light that shows part of the way through the dark, and it can introduce a new vista.

Finding 20 Strengths

When we see teenage patients with a history of drug use and related depression, we can expect them to believe that drugs are their only possible source of pleasure. Because such teens often feel helpless when it comes to healing themselves, we developed a simple exercise that should be required in every home because it builds beneficial brain patterns.

Ask your child to name 20 strengths, such as "I am good in math," "I can throw a football very far," or "I am a good person." Why? Our strengths make us successful in life. The weaknesses we have can help us appreciate others for their unique skills, but in the real world, building on our strengths is usually the key to success.

It only makes good sense to know what those strengths are. Sometimes, though, we are reluctant to acknowledge and develop them. For example, in high school, I participated in sports and band. At 18, I had scholarship offers in both music and football. I was most comfortable as an athlete, so I played college football. When I tried to keep my hand in music by sitting in with a lab jazz band, I was so intimidated that I sold my horn the next day.

Nevertheless, music composition is still a part of my life even as I grow older—and it has helped me to use music and rhythm in therapeutic treatments. Competitive sports are less important to me now, of course. The point is that our strengths may change over time. We suggest naming 20 potential strengths because teenagers' strengths may change, too.

After your child has a list of 20 strengths, instruct him or her to recite these strengths before or after every meal. It is even better to chant the strengths. A neural connection for self-esteem can be created if the list is repeated often and with some fervor; think of the process as adding another plank to the platform of the child's new-and-improved self-image.

Cognitive Psychotherapy for Eliminating Self-Myths in Teen Addicts

Myths are negative constructs that people carry around. They arise from emotions—not facts. Negative constructs can become self-defeating guiding principles based on false premises, such as *I am not worthy of love.* One of the most devilish constructs addicts often carry is a sense of worthlessness. This sense of inadequacy is often tied to frustrated or angry parental criticism such as, "You are a piece of crap, and you'll never amount to anything." I can't tell you how many times I've heard that statement. Parents must help their children understand that such a statement is not true.

Here are seven of the most common myths associated with people stuck in a distressed state, and the reality check that debunks each of them:

- "Everyone must love and respect me."
  Reality check: It is impossible to be loved and respected by everyone, because the world is composed of all sorts of people with a wide variety of opinions, tastes, preferences, and prejudices. It would be far better to focus on extending love and respect to those who truly matter.

- "There is a right and wrong answer to everything."

  Reality check: In every situation, some answers are better than others. Circumstances can change, though, and opinions evolve.

- "It is horrible if things don't turn out as planned."

  Reality check: Nothing is horrible or wonderful. We may see them as terrible or good, but this perception is not always shared by others. Events occur for reasons we sometimes can't understand, and accidents happen.

- "'They' or 'it' makes me feel depressed."

  Reality check: Nothing and no one makes us feel one way or another. We control our own reactions. That is a freedom no one can take from us.

- "I have to be competent and in control of everything I do—or no one will respect me."

  Reality check: People usually respect you because of your courage and efforts—not because of your control.

- "I am the only one following the rules in the game of life."

  Reality check: There are no rules to life, only contracts you make with other people. Unless these contracts are explicit and agreed upon, there are no rules you can apply to anyone but yourself.

- "If I do nothing, happiness will come to me."
  Reality check: Happiness is a by-product of how you consciously choose to live your life. This requires action on your part to not only achieve a happy or positive state of mind, but also to do what it takes to maintain it.

Challenge Destructive Brain Patterns

Teenagers can absolutely, positively replace destructive brain patterns. Using Brain Plasticity Principle II (*Neuron bundles are changed by experience and need*), teenagers can form more constructive thought patterns. An addict does not want to be stuck in a negative mood forever. A distraction that can shift the brain state into a more active mode benefits the brain's overall functioning and improves self-esteem as a bonus. Here are several strategies:

Learning a New Skill or Ability

Although trying to convince someone who is in the depths of despair to concentrate on learning something new can be extremely difficult, this sort of distraction can be a soothing remedy. For example, I bought a wood flute that's musically idiot-proof. Each note is tuned to play a lovely chord. I love to play this instrument for my patients because it always sounds good and never fails to create an air of transcendence. There are other instruments, aided by computer chips, which now work according to similar principles—and they sound great!

If your teenager is stuck in emotional neutral, give them the gift of an idiot-proof musical instrument. Encourage him or her to start playing every day!

Posture

Mental health professionals know (or should know) that body posture influences our emotional state—and it's also an indication of our mental state. For example, if your teenager stands slumped over, chest deflated, eyes cast downward, his or her brain will soon follow, and he or she will begin to feel terrible.

However, if your teenager stands looking straight out onto the world, chest thrust out, with shoulders back and arms spread open like they want to give the world a big hug, it becomes far more difficult to hold on to a negative thought. Of course, no one can maintain that posture indefinitely, but it's a fast and easy tool to get your teenager unstuck.

Psychotherapy and Counseling

As I wrote in an author's note at the beginning of the book, I think innovative home remedies can be useful in many instances, but I recommend psychotherapy and counseling by professionals with training and experience in identifying your child's personal triggers. This is key, because by identifying them, you can develop effective coping mechanisms.

Imagery

One of our greatest gifts is the ability to visualize positive scenarios that help give us relief from our problems. That ability can actually invest your teenager with the power to change his or her physical state. In order to help your child get unstuck from depressive patterns, continue to suggest that he or she unload negative burdens. There *are* ways to build new connections in the mind. Here are some more suggestions for your teenager to get his or her creative juices flowing:

- Visualize emptying all your problems and regrets in a bag and then dumping the bag into the ocean. Watch it sink to the bottom—leaving you free!

- Write the problems that are keeping you from changing on a piece of paper, and then fold it up. Then, in a fire-safe environment (like in a fireplace), burn the paper. Let the problems disintegrate.

- Make a prayer stick. Write blessings on small pieces of paper and tie them on a stick 16 to 24 inches long and about a half inch in diameter. Wrap the stick with your favorite colored yarn and decorate it with one or two of your treasured objects. This becomes your prayer stick; it symbolizes the blessings you seek.

- Draw pictures of your problem areas. Then destroy the pictures—or paint over them with new drawings of your goals and hopes. Use a lot of detail.

- Dance out the act of casting off your negative thoughts and bringing in the blessings you want, and rejoice.

Exercise and Rhythm

Research in psychology and medicine reveals that exercise is a great weapon against the effects of anxiety and depression caused by addiction. Through the expansion and contraction of muscles, the coordinated effort of breathing, and the increased energy outlay of the body, many mental problems are resolved. Depression relief through exercise can be more effective than some medications, and it's great for relaxing many anxieties. Exercise can also aid with emotional stability and inspire better performance in other areas of life.

There is nothing negative that can be said about the use of exercise in proper amounts, except that for many it can be boring. Some take exercise to an extreme, of course, and that can result in injury to muscles and joints. There is an optimal exercise level for most people; extreme amounts of exercise can create internal cravings and addiction-like dynamics triggered by our bodies' natural painkillers, known as *endorphins*. For these reasons, I've offered a few guidelines:

- Exercise needs to be rhythmic in nature so that the motion of the body coordinates with the rhythm of the organs, muscles, brain cells, sensory inputs, and so on. For example, walking, jogging, running, and swimming are all good exercises because they have a coordinated pace.

- Exercise activities like Zumba that incorporate music are also beneficial because of their rhythmic nature.

- Exercise with a friend is a great option because two or more people are combining their energies and motions. Exercise classes sometimes have an advantage over individual efforts, and ballroom dancing offers a whole new level of enjoyment—as well as mental health benefits. Participating in exercise of any kind with your teenager can provide great bonding experiences, too!

Get Support for Yourself

Parents who feel their child may be depressed from drug or alcohol abuse should reach out for support for themselves. Too often, parents shut themselves off from the outside world. Instead, plan an event with your child—and take some friends! Go on a trip. Visit someplace new, exciting, and different. A change of scenery can change everyone's vision and perceptions—and the support of friends and those who care for you can make the events more meaningful.

CHAPTER SEVEN

TREATING YOUR ADDICTED TEENAGER'S OBSESSIVE CRAVING

Jared was a typical 15-year-old, a good-looking boy who had been suffering from grief over the loss of his best friend. But in this instance, his "best friend" was pot. Jared had found the strength to give up marijuana, but he felt as though he had lost part of his life. He was obsessed with his memory of pot as a cure for his anxieties—and this obsession was nearly as damaging as the pot itself had been. Jared's grades were suffering, too, which only added to his anxiety levels.

Jared was the third child in an ambitious family. His older brother was a leader in academics and sports, sought after by executive recruiters even before college graduation. He received most of his parents' attention and was held up as a role model for his siblings. Jared's older sister demonstrated her leadership more in social clubs and organizations. By age 17, she was involved with various national volunteer organizations and received scholarships for her superb administration and organizational skills.

Jared was intimidated by the tough acts he had to follow. He was smart enough, but he felt he lacked leadership qualities. His parents told him that in order to prove himself as a leader, he had to have someone willing to follow him. A natural introvert, he found it difficult enough to make friends, much less to step up as a leader. So under pressure to prove his mettle, Jared set out to *buy* some friends.

In middle school, Jared gave $5 to classmates for hanging out with him each day. Soon, the number of "friends" on his payroll was growing daily, which added to his expenses. His biggest fear was that his mom and dad would find out about him paying off his peers. Stealing money from his parents was easy enough for the first few months, but as the list of paid friends grew, Jared's anxiety increased. He was having nightmares because of his precarious situation.

Jared did manage to find a group of friends who weren't on the dole. They actually seemed to care about him. But they convinced him that smoking pot made him cooler and more of a leader. At first, they gave him pot, and Jared convinced himself that he had been accepted. Pot served as a calming medicine, and his anxieties eased. Soon enough, however, Jared's new group of friends began charging for his "medicine," although this cost less than his former payroll, so he didn't have to steal money from home as often. It wasn't long, though, before Jared's parents began to notice that he had become disrespectful and irresponsible. Drug testing, which I recommend to any parent who suspects their teenager is abusing drugs, confirmed their suspicions.

The Brain Model of Craving

Addictive drugs have the power to control pleasure-seeking neurological patterns and to eliminate other patterns that might compete with these commanding forces. As the balance of frequency levels and patterns of neurons fluctuate, the brain becomes disorganized. It's similar to a school marching band that suddenly loses its director.

The *anterior cingulate cortex* (ACC) wraps around a thick, fibrous nerve bundle that connects the brain's two hemispheres. Believed to be the center for cognitive functions, the ACC is responsible for focusing and coordinating different parts of the brain for optimal problem solving, and governs the ability to have empathy for others and their emotions. When the ACC is no longer serving to organize the brain, the ability to resolve problems or manage cravings is lost. Brain patterns are scrambled, and cravings are unregulated and constant.

The ACC's role in new memory storage may also explain why its function is associated with post-traumatic stress disorder (PTSD). When people experience a traumatic event and their ACC is damaged, their brains replay events over and over instead of presenting them as memories that fade over time. This concept may also help explain the repetitive obsessive memories in obsessive-compulsive disorders. For example, if a person keeps repeatedly checking the door locks, this is because the memory of performing the task is somehow repeatedly deleted as well. Thus, the brain insists that the task must be performed again and again.

Obsessive Pattern Assessment

Below is a list of symptoms that may help you confirm a diagnosis of obsessive brain patterns. Count how many of these statements apply to your teenager—not just occasionally, but on most days.

1. Your child has intrusive, persistent thoughts and images that trigger anxiety and stress, often interfering with day-to-day functioning.

2. Your child attempts unsuccessfully to ignore intrusive thoughts.

3. Your child attempts to control intrusive thoughts through repetitive behaviors.

4. Your child is driven at all costs to reduce the resulting anxiety and frustration that results from intrusive thoughts and images.

5. Your child feels the irrational compulsion to perform certain activities, such as washing hands or counting, as a means to reduce anxiety.

6. Your child is spending at least an hour each day dealing with intrusive thoughts and images.

7. Your child often feels depressed because of the persistent memories of regret and disillusionment.

8. Your child cannot control or diminish the intensity of negative thoughts or images triggered by external events.

9. Your child tries to achieve perfection in an attempt to avoid criticism, anxiety, and frustration.

10. Your child is rigid in the performance of daily routines in an attempt to maintain control over the intrusion of negative thoughts and images that trigger anxiety.

11. Your child is stressed and anxious because he or she cannot stop thinking about cravings.

12. Your child is not satisfied until each task is perfectly completed.

13. Your child is often consumed by guilt, frequently for no discernible reason.

14. Your child cannot release problems of the past that have been long forgiven and forgotten.

Scoring: If eight or more of these statements apply, there is a reasonable chance that your teenager's brain is vulnerable to stress-inducing patterns. Such persistent internal conflict isn't good for the brain, body, or spirit.

Methods for Shifting Obsessive Craving Patterns

As we've seen, the brain can change; destructive brain patterns can be altered and new patterns created that produce healthier outcomes. Prayer, for example, can have a positive impact on brain patterns. I've witnessed Navajo prayer healing and forgiveness rituals that have helped both individuals and entire communities.

How this works is far beyond my understanding. Because I have no objective models to understand or evaluate these methods, I don't cast judgment upon them. But if these rituals work (and they certainly do for some people), who am I to deny their success?

I am, however, a scientist at heart. So, for the most part, claims of cures from isolated incidents don't wash with me. Whenever possible, I believe it is important to test theories and replicate results.

The following are methods and protocols that have worked for many people who suffer from obsessive, cyclonic brain stress. Remember: using Brain Plasticity Principle II (*Neuron bundles are changed by experience and need*), we can create spaces in brain processes for the new pathways.

Using the BAUD
(BioAcoustical Utilization Device)

As mentioned earlier, the BAUD is a device that uses sound frequencies to change brain patterns. I have found it useful for interrupting cravings and other obsessive types of brain patterns, such as phobias and PTSD.

Basically, the patient dons headphones connected to the device and then finds the frequency that is closely associated with the disturbing images or thoughts. This is called the "sympathetic frequency" and is related to the sympathetic system of arousal. To find it, the patient adjusts the frequency levels in each ear until he or she feels a heightened level of emotion (more fear or anxiousness, for example).

Listening to these two frequencies, a different one in each ear, simultaneously allows a third frequency to be generated deep within the brain—a phenomenon called the *binaural beat*. This disrupts the sympathetic frequency and pauses the anxiety associated with the lack of brain coordination and returns it to a parasympathetic state.

Once anxiety stops, the patient spends a few minutes breathing and relaxing. This calms the formerly high state of chaos in the brain and releases the intensity of cravings and obsessions. If the session is successful, the brain still experiences pleasure, but without drugs. While the BAUD does not work for everyone, many people have had remarkable success with it, both at our treatment centers and at home. For more information, visit www.MyBAUD.com.

"Progressive Muscle Relaxation" Audio Program

The second audio in my MindBody Anxiety Relief program offers drumming rhythms recorded at my house. This recording has proved the most effective in treating obsessive cravings and appears to take hold over a period of two to four weeks. The audio features a 22-minute drumming session set at a low-beta frequency—the most powerful learning frequencies for the brain. (For more information, visit www.MindBody Series.com.)

Breath Control

Alternate nostril breathing is a yoga breathing technique that involves inhaling through one nostril at a time. Some may scoff at the idea, but I have some impressive brain scans to support my conclusion that this breathing tool has therapeutic value. My patients have successfully used this nostril-breathing technique to halt intrusive, obsessive thoughts. There are a few different versions of this technique, but the following is the most simple of them.

Have your teenager gently press his or her index finger against the right nostril so that it is blocked. He or she should inhale and exhale slowly and purposefully, and then switch nostrils. This alternate nostril breathing should be continued until a sense of calm is restored. Then, he or she should continue for an additional six minutes—three minutes per nostril.

Distraction Directives

Just as the brain can be trained with rhythms, it is also susceptible to verbal distractions. Use the following script if your child appears to be going through an obsessive episode. Ask your teenager to choose a place where he or she can be comfortable and won't be disturbed. The best place may even be a closet or a bathroom. Turn off all cell phones. Both of you should get into a comfortable position where you won't be shifting around. You will be focusing your attention on your breathing. Once you are in place and settled, say the following:

I want you to slowly close your eyes. This helps you to concentrate. Take a deep breath and hold it for a second. Now, let out the breath with an even flow of air as I count to seven. 1 – 2 – 3 – 4 – 5 – 6 – 7. Good. Now breathe in to the same count. 1 – 2 – 3 – 4 – 5 – 6 – 7. Now out: 1 – 2 – 3 – 4 – 5 – 6 – 7. Now in: 1 – 2 – 3 – 4 – 5 – 6 – 7. Now out: 1 – 2 – 3 – 4 – 5 – 6 – 7. Now in: 1 – 2 – 3 – 4 – 5 – 6 – 7.

Now out. While you are breathing out, let yourself feel more relaxed. Let go of any stress with your breath. Now in. Breathe in the good things that heal you and make you stronger. Now out: 1 – 2 – 3 – 4 – 5 – 6 – 7. Now in: 1 – 2 – 3 – 4 – 5 – 6 – 7. Now out. You may feel yourself getting dizzy, and that is okay. You are changing your brain patterns. Now in: Learn to accept yourself as perfect. Now out: Let yourself release and relax.

Now in: You are becoming very relaxed. Let your brain relax. Now out: You are feeling relaxed; you are very relaxed; you are relaxed and safe; there's nothing to worry about. Now in: 1 – 2 – 3 – 4 – 5 – 6 – 7. Now out: 1 – 2 – 3 – 4 – 5 – 6 – 7. In: 1 – 2 – 3 – 4 – 5 – 6 – 7. Out: 1 – 2 – 3 – 4 – 5 – 6 – 7. Now continue breathing in this pattern, and count silently to yourself as you breathe.

"Catching" the emWave Desktop

The emWave Desktop is a biofeedback system that includes both a heart-rate monitor and software for your computer. The emWave can help the user create synchronized brain waves and balanced emotions by collecting pulse data and, through various exercises disguised as fun computer games, teaching how to bring the heart and mind into a coherent state for an extended period of time. (For more information, visit www.heartmathstore.com.)

Neurotherapy

Neurotherapy is a professionally administered therapy that is often successful in stabilizing the chaotic brains of addicts. With the help of a trained therapist, patients can learn ways of balancing discordant brain frequencies to reduce stress, ADD/ADHD symptoms, and obsessive cravings. A therapists trained in electro-encephalograph (EEG) technology attaches Band-Aid-like sensors to the patient's scalp so that the patient's brain waves can be recorded during the session. The EEG monitor serves as an emotional mirror, and the therapist can see small changes resulting from the patient's imagery, breathing, attitude, and so on. The therapist teaches the patient how to read the graphs generated by the EEG on a monitor and how to recognize the desired range. Through this feedback, the patient can learn to affect the brain immediately and directly. This method takes time, but it's probably the most direct way to permanently alter brain waves.

Mindfulness Meditation

Mindfulness meditation is considered one of the best exercises to control obsessions, ruminations, and anxiety. I am a big fan of this exercise, which is really more of a philosophy about our real control over life and the discipline of maintaining a focus on what is real versus what is unreal. With the mind fully engaged in a minute-to-minute awareness of a person's experience without judgment, the person interacts within the boundaries of relevant values. In this sense, mindfulness is a state that promotes a keen awareness of what is and is not important.

As an exercise, mindfulness involves a person focusing on becoming relaxed but not unaware or numb to experiences and thoughts. The goal is to focus awareness totally in the present, excluding any thoughts of the past or future. The philosophy is that you cannot change the past and do not know the future—the only relevancy is what is going on right now. By focusing on one's own reality and experience, the mind is relieved of nonessential thoughts. Moreover, because it is not distracted with the past and the future, the mind can be *allowed* to reveal deeper meaning underlying life experiences, thereby granting greater wisdom.

Through learning to focus attention and awareness and to bring thoughts under greater voluntary control, mindfulness fosters general mental well-being as well as calmness, clarity, and concentration. Studies have shown that mindfulness meditation can reduce stress and rumination (obsessive worry thoughts) and boost working memory, concentration, creativity, and compassion. Mindful meditation practice is critical for healing because the destructive chaos of obsessions requires discipline to banish.

There are few rules for mindfulness meditation. Generally, the process is conducted in pairs. Periodically, one member of the pair asks, "What is happening now? What am I feeling now? What is the experience right now?" These questions are used not to solicit answers, but to aid in tracking each person's attention and to help prevent distracted thinking. Love and support are always projected.

Rhythmic Exercise

Rhythmic exercise is dancing within a specific tempo. Dancing creates a unique mental state and helps foster brain frequencies associated with joy. The late Dr. Carl Simonton (a renowned oncologist) and I used to work with very ill cancer patients. As we approached one specific session, I asked if I could try music and drumming for the patients. Carl was always looking for new ways to help his patients, and we agreed on a one-hour session.

I told the patients to move in concert with the music in whatever way they could—even if they just sat and moved their bodies from a chair. I thought that many of the patients would get tired after just 30 minutes, but as we reached that time limit, everyone who could was still standing and their energy was building. The impact was so powerful that dancing became a nightly ritual. Virtually all the patients felt healthier, and some even became convinced that their tumors were disappearing because of the powerful peaceful energy they felt.

Other groups I've worked with have benefited from dance therapy, including the elderly, chronic-pain patient groups, cancer support groups, and patients with stress issues.

Chanting

Just as the brain responds to music and rhythm, it also responds (even more so, in fact) to the internal vibrations made by our own vocal cords. Chanting in repetition has been shown to shift the overall brain frequency toward alpha (which is the relaxation range), creating a harmonious state and helping the person chanting to feel more peaceful and confident.

It's all quantum physics, actually. All particles—including atoms, electrons and subatomic particles—are energy in a state of vibration. Since sound is a vibration, we can assume that anything that generates it will cause other particles to act as resonators, picking up the sound from the source. (Think of a tuning fork.) This change in the vibration of subatomic particles can impact the structure of atoms and cells—especially if the vibration comes from within the body.

The words used as mantras or inspirational sentences in chanting can have a big influence. It's well accepted that destructive phrases ("I'm a total idiot," "I don't deserve good things," "I'm a bad person," or "I'm sinful") can create negative brain patterns. Likewise, positive phrases can create positive brain patterns if practiced consistently. I usually require those dealing with addiction to repeat a positive phrase 1,000 times a day in order to combat negative thoughts. Remember: neurons that fire together, wire together.

I recommend your teenager start by choosing one phrase, such as "I can do this" or "I am enough," to use as their chanting phrase. Spiritual phrases, like "God loves me," "I am forgiven," or "God walks with me," have shown excellent results as well. In my therapeutic interactions, I've chosen specific phrases that pertain to a patient's unique needs and brain function. I recommend you do the same and help your teenager choose what's right for him or her.

Parents can encourage their children to use these phrases by modeling them themselves. You might make a pledge to lower your intake of sugar or alcohol and then use the same chanting methods as therapy—with your child watching. This can also help the teen feel less alone, as someone in need of special treatment. Sometimes being "the problem child" is a very isolating experience. If you undergo your own self-therapy, it gives you and your child something to discuss and share.

Psychotherapy and Counseling

Your teenager's obsessive cravings will not cease unless his or her psychological triggers are recognized and resolved. An addict's cravings can be triggered by seemingly benign cues, and the responses can be immediate and difficult to control. The best way to control cravings is to recognize warning signs and cut off the response.

With Jared, the boy whose story I shared at the beginning of this chapter, the major issue was that he felt he didn't measure up to his family's expectation that he would become a leader. Jared had to become aware of his cues and reroute his psychological responses to more constructive patterns. Jared discovered that in truth, neither he *nor* his accomplished siblings could live up to their parents' expectations. He announced that he was not going to let those expectations rule his life—which paved the way for all three siblings to stage a bit of a rebellion.

In response, their parents shared with them that they, too, had been trapped by the expectations of their own parents. Brain training to help the entire family adjust to a new philosophy was necessary. Jared led the way, bringing the entire family together for dance therapy and mindfulness meditation. It was wonderful to see the family come together, understanding and supporting each other.

Often, a therapist can help make these transitions to a more collaborative and empathetic approach less daunting. Psychotherapy is merely the process of seeking and acknowledging truth. Only when anxiety and depression are relieved will truth and love emerge.

Psychotherapy and counseling for anxiety management can clear the way for emotional growth and relieve the brain affected by addiction. When an addicted child learns to take responsibility for his or her responses to feelings and emotions, many of the traps are removed from the recovery process.

✦ ✦ ✦

CHAPTER EIGHT

Tough Love—When Enough Is Enough

There are cases of teenage addiction and drug and alcohol abuse in which normal therapeutic approaches don't work. I've often seen parents who don't want to confront their addicted teenager's self-destructive behavior even after a parade of therapists, counselors, physicians, and teachers have advised them to take stronger measures.

You may reach a point when your only alternative is "tough love." This is a no-nonsense approach to a very serious challenge. In some instances, the emphasis on "tough" has been overdone. I consider *love* to be the key word in the phrase, and the necessary focus for constructive and lasting change in your child's behavior. Threats, angry words, and punishment *do not* have to be part of this therapeutic approach. Granted, the child may have developed some highly manipulative behavior patterns, but you can remain focused on acting out of love—with a strong spiritual emphasis.

A tough-love approach will help you become a better parent. It will bring you to your knees if you insist on demanding that your child meet rigid standards of performance. You must prepare yourself for a new way of parenting, loving your child, and knowing your God in a more personal way.

Thy Will Be Done

In a tough-love intervention, parents must learn to trust the process for the good of the child. This is unselfish love in action. You must give up on seeking personal rewards, such as apologies from your child or repayment for damage done. The goal is for your child to recognize his or her destructive behavior and to change in order to stop using drugs and alcohol. You can't withhold love or deny love from your child because of the addiction. This makes your love conditional rather than unconditional—and conditional love is more about self-interest than selflessness. If you feel any of the following emotions while working with your child to overcome addiction, you'll likely need to resolve issues in your relationship:

Embarrassment	Rejection
Rationalization	Rage or panic
Fear	Constant worry
Anxiety	Hostility toward
Guilt	health care
Isolation	Hopelessness
Anger	Self-pity
Disgust	Vindictiveness
Protectiveness	Unwillingness to
Pity or sympathy	communicate
Preoccupation with	Rigidity
addiction	

Many approaches can help you achieve better rapport with an addicted child. One of the simplest is writing shared journal entries. This works because it eliminates overwrought emotions that can compromise discussions. To do this, you simply write a note, addressed to your teenager, about the issue you want to discuss. Encourage your child to read your note silently and then aloud. Then ask him or her to explain your note. The idea isn't to convince the child that you are right as much as it is for the child to understand the issues and your point of view. Agreement can come later.

Then ask your teenager to write a reply. Read your teenager's note silently and then aloud, and then explain to your teenager what you just read. Repeat the process until a mutual understanding is reached. The process is slow, but that is the intent, as you are trying to slow the emotional reactions so the communications can proceed.

Structured Intervention

In its simplest form, intervention with drug and alcohol addicts happens each time the child is confronted. Such intervention is usually inadequate and counterproductive. The addictive behavior doesn't change following such an encounter, and it may even worsen, creating more anger and frustration for family and friends. Indeed, constant confrontation—what I call *regular intervention*—often isolates the addict.

The difference between a regular intervention and a more structured intervention is that the latter adheres to a specific format. In structured intervention, family, friends, and teachers of the chemically dependent teenager come together as a group to confront the addict and interrupt the addicted brain's habitual defenses and responses. A structured intervention is based on the tenets of Brain Plasticity Principle II (*Neuron bundles are changed by experience and need*).

A tough-love intervention process requires a strong commitment from the intervention team. The team must put together a very precise and powerful strategy. Like a surgical team, the leaders are usually professionals, who have a plan of action for disrupting and replacing the addictive behavior patterns. Other team members include selected family members and friends who have the power to influence the addict's behavior.

The best resources for intervention training come from the Association of Intervention Specialist Certification Board (www.aiscb.org) and the ARISE Intervention Model and Certification Program (www.linkinghuman systems.com/arise).

Why Intervene?

Alcoholism and drug abuse is (when left untreated) a progressive and terminal disease characterized by delusion and denial. Without help, an addicted teenager is doomed, because the brain has been reprogrammed to serve the craving first and foremost, resulting in an inevitable mental, physical, and emotional downward spiral. A diseased brain makes addicts oblivious to all consequences or realities beyond the pleasure provided, however briefly, by drugs. An addict is focused only on serving the craving. Nothing else matters. No other purpose or goal is worthy of consideration.

Adult addicts who are legally responsible for their own behavior may respond only after "hitting bottom." But parents and guardians of teenagers cannot wait. An intervention serves to "raise the bottom" and create the crisis, breaking through the denial system and leading the child to potential recovery. An intervention can also promote cooperation from the addict. Intervention works on several different levels: neurologically, biologically, psychologically, and spiritually.

In a structured intervention, certain elements *must* be present. It is essential that two or more caring and concerned people are willing to nonjudgmentally confront the addict. An intervention is often rehearsed so that everyone is well versed in their roles. Each participant must be willing to take risks necessary to help the child. An intervention is a carefully orchestrated and controlled event in which virtually nothing is left to chance and all potential outcomes are anticipated. There is much to do to prepare for a structured intervention. Ideally, the intervention-training program will consist of an assessment interview, three team-development classes, the intervention, and a follow-up accountability session.

Assessment Session

An assessment interview is a meeting for all interveners to determine what resources are needed for the best approach. For example, someone may have provided guidance to the addict in the past, but the team needs to evaluate whether that individual is likely to be strong and not an enabler during the intervention. Those on the team must be unified in their goal of interrupting brain patterns long enough to introduce new ones. The messages must be clear, practical, and consistent from one member to the next.

There are basic rules for an intervention force. These include:

- Being responsible for attending the teaching sessions, intervention, and follow-up sessions

- Maintaining the privacy and confidentiality of the total force organization and the events as they occur (trust is essential)

- Being honest, genuine, and accurate with any information you share

- Agreeing not to use drugs or alcohol during the intervention periods

You also have rights as part of the intervention force. Remember, too, that an intervention is often a life-changing event for the addict and for the members of the intervention team. Your rights include:

- The right to expect respect and consideration of your feelings

- The right to privacy

- The right to request and receive information about the reasons and goals for the intervention

- The right to contact your intervention facilitator at any time if you need to express yourself or gain critical information about the process

- The right to file a complaint to a certifying board if you feel your rights have been violated

Team Development Class #1

There are five goals for Team Development Class #1:

- To gain a thorough understanding of addiction and its consequences

- To gain group cohesion

- To review intervention guidelines and the best way to reach the addict

- To discuss various avenues for treatment, such as inpatient or outpatient treatment, therapy options, and the social structure provided by each

- To make decisions about the date and location of the structured intervention

In reviewing the options for treatment, there are several considerations. Inpatient programs offer control; outpatient programs offer freedom and rely on more of a collaborative effort with family members. These often require frequent drug testing, a curfew, and participation in AA or drug-addiction programs with sponsor check-ins.

Team Development Class #2

The focus of Team Development Class #2 is the role of the family in the development of the addictive behavior. No blame is assigned; blame is not productive and can only serve to further divide a family. Family-oriented enabling behavior is identified and discussed to prepare for the teenager's future relationships and environments. Class #2 should also spend time anticipating responses from the addict and preparing responses from the intervention force. Rehearsal of scenarios might also be helpful.

In-depth discussions about family dynamics may include specifying roles for each member in the intervention. For example, one family member should serve as "peacemaker" and facilitator among the group. Another person often serves as a family leader or hero figure who is widely respected inside and outside the family. A family member who provides humor and eases tension is another common role. By identifying roles for family and team members, the group allows each member to play to his or her strengths in the intervention.

Once the intervention team agrees on the treatment decisions and what roles the team members will have, I recommend that family members start attending meetings of Al-Anon, a group developed by Alcoholics Anonymous specifically for family members of alcoholics.

Team Development Class #3

Practical considerations in anticipation of confrontation should be discussed during Team Development

Class #3. Are all members of the team comfortable with the anticipated reactions from the addict? Are all responses from the team rehearsed? Every team member should be in agreement with the plan and its goals. The team should once again confirm a meeting place and time.

Intervention Session

Then comes the actual intervention. The intervention force and intervention facilitator confront the addicted teenager and proceed with the structured intervention. The goals are to confront the teenager with the facts of the addiction and with his or her self-destructive and unacceptable behavior, to explain the illness, and to make plans to stop this downward spiral. Always maintain a spirit of love and concern during each step. The cardinal rules for a structured intervention include care, concern, and support.

During a typical structured intervention, the facilitator opens with an introduction and an immediate declaration that everyone is participating because they are concerned about the addict's emotional and physical health. The facilitator explains that the group members will each express their thoughts and concerns, and asks the teenager for a verbal commitment to stay for the intervention. The facilitator then explains that each team member must be allowed to speak without interruption, and the teenager will be given the opportunity to respond in turn. Events and activities discussed during the intervention are only those related to addiction; otherwise, the meeting could become disorganized and confusing. There should be no accusatory or condemning language, such as calling the teenager an "alcoholic," "drug addict," or "druggie." Such language can make the teen defensive and fearful.

During the intervention, each team member must be clear and concise as they confront the addict. It is helpful to discuss the time and place of incidents related to the addict's behavior, and witnesses to events should be mentioned to avoid denial. These facts are presented to the teenager to demonstrate the behavior patterns and explain why the family is concerned. The emphasis shouldn't be on debating specific events but instead on overall concerns. If the teenager disagrees with the facts presented, the team should provide reassurance of its desire only to reach understanding and to help the child.

After the presentations of facts, a facilitator will state that the addict needs professional help to break the self-destructive behavior patterns and end the downward spiral. Based on the earlier discussions in the classes, the facilitator will likely offer a recommended choice for treatment. Questions from the child as well as the concerned group may be entertained, but a final plan must be set.

In the case of a minor, parents will have to approve the final decision. Based on the resources available, a facilitator may offer several options. At the very least, however, a program must be selected and presented to the addict that will help get him or her on the road toward a healthy life.

Follow-up Session

As quickly as possible after the intervention is concluded, the team should meet to discuss the outcome of the intervention, how they feel about it, and how comfortable they were with the teenager's response. Each force member may play a role in helping the teenager stay with the program, particularly if the teen will be receiving outpatient treatment.

The 12-Step Program

During either in- or outpatient treatment, your teenager will more than likely be introduced to the 12-step program, a step-by-step transformational process introduced by Alcoholics Anonymous co-founders Bill Wilson and Dr. Bob Smith. Millions of recovering addicts credit the 12 steps as a major factor in their efforts to achieve sobriety.

In 1939, Wilson, a recovering alcoholic, wrote *The Big Book,* a guide to sober living founded on strong spiritual concepts that includes the 12 steps. Steering clear of traditional religious dogma, he relied on personal definitions of God and discipline as the guideposts for ethical behaviors while working toward a state of sobriety. He believed group support in a casual setting is critical for the addict in creating a sense of acceptance, understanding, and community.

These well-founded principles have not changed over the years. The 12-step method deserves its due; it has been the most effective addiction program in the world. No one would argue its importance or the relevance of its role. That said, AA's strength is also its limitation. It is a one-dimensional approach, and it may not apply to every person.

The program offers a transformational process for everybody, including family members, because the program teaches that everyone touched by the addict is affected—and must change. For example, if drinking alcohol has traditionally been the family's way of dealing with stress, that behavior and any other enabling behaviors need to change when the addict returns home after completing a program.

I recommend that every family member and loved one become familiar with The 12 steps. Addiction is a family problem—and it takes a family to turn the issues around. Here is an overview of the steps:

1. We admitted we were powerless over (addictive substances)—that our lives had become unmanageable.

I often ask families if any members have the answer or method to deal with the child's addiction. Usually there is no response, but I can feel the desperation and I see the slumped shoulders. I ask this to make the point that whatever the family has tried to do isn't working. Professional guidance is needed. Denial is often a major obstacle for both addict and family alike. Most families simply don't have all the tools needed to defeat a loved one's addiction issues.

2. We came to believe that a power greater than ourselves could restore us to sanity.

A greater power usually means a spiritual force of some kind, such as love and compassion, rather than intellect or some form of discipline of thought. Addiction is a disease of distorted mental motivations, and the only way to deal with it is through hope and faith.

3. We made a decision to turn our will and our lives over to the care of God as we understood Him.

The phrase "as we understood Him" makes this step more applicable to all spiritual beliefs. It does make sense that higher forms of learning are required to love your child and to help him or her get beyond addictive behavior. It takes spiritual strength to deal with someone you love who is in the throes of addiction.

4. We made a searching and fearless moral inventory of ourselves.

In most cases of addiction, many contributing factors exist, including family dynamics. As the addict has to look within and take an honest assessment of his or her actions, the addicted teenager's family needs to look within and see how they can change for the health of the child and family.

5. We admitted to God, to ourselves, and to another human being the exact nature of our wrongs.

This step involves sharing the inventory with another person who is supportive, not shaming. While it takes courage to express these things, it is part of owning responsibility. Secrecy is part of the disease. Talking openly and honestly, on the other hand, is a move toward healing.

6. We were entirely ready to have God remove all these defects of character.

In some situations, *spiritual* forgiveness is the only avenue of forgiveness.

7. We humbly asked Him to remove our shortcomings.

As in any prayer, this step is about asking for help from a higher power, whoever or whatever that might be.

8. We made a list of all persons we had harmed, and became willing to make amends to them all.

Regardless of how much we have tried not to do so, each of us has made mistakes and hurt others in our lives. As your teenager engages with this step and learns to take responsibility, it makes sense for you to do so as well.

9. We made direct amends to such people wherever possible, except when to do so would injure them or others.

This vital step is fairly self-explanatory. As with the step before it, you will find that if you do this along with your addicted teenager, you will not only be supporting your child in leading by example, but you will no doubt greatly benefit yourself.

10. We continued to take personal inventory, and when we were wrong, promptly admitted it.

This step is about continuing the previous steps as time goes on, so that the addict learns that honest self-reflection, staying humble and asking for help, and taking responsibility for one's actions is a continual process and indeed a way of life.

11. We sought through prayer and meditation to improve our conscious contact with God as we understood Him, praying only for knowledge of His will for us and the power to carry that out.

As with the previous step, step 11 is a continuation of those that have come before—in this case, specifically to deepen the connection to one's higher power, whoever or whatever that might be, as a way of life.

12. Having had a spiritual awakening as the result of these steps, we tried to carry this message to alcoholics and to practice these principles in all our affairs.

This step is about two very powerful principles—first, that reaching out to help others should be a natural part of life (and that extending such help also greatly benefits the person offering assistance); and second, that successful recovery demands that the addict adopt these guidelines in *all* areas of his or her life (for example, being honest about drinking and drug use, as well as about everything else).

A Note of Caution

The material in this chapter has offered brief descriptions of a very complicated process. Not only is addiction and its aftermath an extremely emotional ordeal, but drugs and alcohol can destroy a teenager's ability to process and retain information. For these reasons and others, interventions are neither quick nor easy. Although an intervention plan is your best bet for helping your child mature in outlook and perception, the process takes time. A structured intervention is only the beginning of the transformation in family dynamics. Be prepared for a struggle, but have hope, courage, and faith in the benevolent power of love. One day, you may look back with pride on how your family responded and came together in this crisis. It is certainly all worth it.

PART IV

HEALING RELATIONSHIPS AND SPIRITS

CHAPTER NINE

MENDING RELATIONSHIPS AMONG THE TEENAGE ADDICT AND FAMILY MEMBERS

At age 14, Nancy was highly vulnerable to addictive behavior due to turmoil in her family. Her parents had recently divorced after a volatile breakup in which both sides blamed each other for their unhappiness. Nancy had no close friends. She had little interest in the usual teenage social interactions. She avoided discussing her feelings or personal issues. She was too embarrassed to talk about family problems that might have explained her dark moods. She didn't want to listen to other girls talk about family matters because she was ashamed of her own. Nancy was emotionally withdrawn at school.

One day, an older boy offered Nancy an escape from her emotional pain. She was leaning on a fence during gym class when he approached her. Soon, Nancy was addicted to drugs. She knew the dangers, but she was so depressed and lonely that his offer of companionship overcame her wariness. She was also so unhappy that she felt things couldn't get any worse. That afternoon, Nancy laughed for the first time in quite a while. It felt good.

With pleasure comes possibility, and Nancy found this boy and his friends exciting. She began with pot, but this lead to more drugs. Nancy was soon using Adderall, which gave her energy like she had never felt before. Her new friends taught her how easy it was to get Adderall. They told her to convince her mother that she had attention deficit disorder, providing her with exactly what she needed to say to convince her parents and her doctor to write a prescription. Nancy followed the script, telling her mother she couldn't focus on her schoolwork and was falling behind in classes. She said other kids told her that Adderall would help her.

Nancy's mother didn't buy the story. She took her daughter to a clinical psychologist for a full evaluation. The psychologist quickly realized the game Nancy was trying to play and began treating her real problems. The psychologist diagnosed her primary challenges as depression and adjustment disorder, an inability to cope with stressful events or situations.

The psychologist suggested family therapy with her divorced parents as a first step. The process proved successful for the whole family, and communication became a priority. The therapist encouraged Nancy and assisted her in forming stronger bonds with her divorced parents. The guidance counselor and the softball coach helped Nancy find healthier ways of dealing with her depression through school activities and sports. Nancy also experienced a renewal of religious faith and began making new friends through her church.

Nancy found she didn't need drugs to deal with stressful things in her life. Her family, friends, and faith filled the need that the drugs had addressed. She found that life without drugs was better, and although she remained friends with some of the "druggies," she did not join them in smoking pot or taking pills. She became such a good softball player that she earned a college athletic scholarship, which took her on an exciting new path that she'd never thought possible.

This sort of success story is fairly common. There are resources available that can save young people from the burden of addiction. Nancy deserves credit for turning her life away from drugs, and so do those who stepped up to guide her back to a more positive path. Those who supported and encouraged Nancy showed her the power of loving and caring relationships.

The following questionnaire is designed to help parents understand why teenagers turn to drugs. Parents often say, "We give our children everything! Why do they do drugs?" The goal of this questionnaire is to give you insight. Grab a notepad and answer each statement with *True* or *False*.

1. Teenagers start taking drugs because they are not happy.

2. Television influences a teenager's use of drugs.

3. Home cooking can influence whether or not a teenager will get involved with drugs.

4. Children who start taking drugs have no plans and goals.

5. Listening to or playing music makes a difference in the attitudes of those using drugs.

6. Some medications for anxiety and depression can inhibit learning and judgment—which can lead to drug use.

7. Allowing your teenager to vent anger can prevent drug use.

8. Parents who use the same discipline methods that *their* parents used will help a teenager feel connected to his or her family and uninterested in drugs.

9. Teenagers start drugs when their wants and desires are not fulfilled.

10. Teenagers are more confident and comforted when their parents breathe slowly.

11. A teenager's ability to walk away from drugs depends, to some degree, on having a healthy brain.

12. The best time to confront a teenager using drugs is when he or she is under the influence.

13. Offering compliments and rewards for good behavior is not effective because teenagers should know how to behave.

14. Corporal punishment is an effective way of dealing with drug behavior.

15. A permissive parenting style encourages a teenager to feel confident.

Scoring:

1. *False.* Yes, teenagers who take drugs are often not happy, but more to the point, they are *confused.* No child grows up wanting to be an alcoholic or drug addict! Unfortunately, some teenagers are simply more intent on feeling pleasure *now* than thinking about their futures.

2. *True.* Television programs and commercials can glorify drug use or, at the very least, make it seem like an acceptable alternative to problem solving and conflict resolution.

3. *True.* A teenager receives more than physical nutrition from a home-cooked meal. When a family gathers for meals, the teen receives needed attention, a stronger sense of family, and the security of a support structure. Values are incredibly important, and the most popular place for parents to express them is at the dinner table. Cooking for your children also helps to convey your love and support.

4. *False.* Teenagers almost always have plans and goals, but they don't always have ways to fulfill them. The problem is often that a teenager's ability to deal with frustrations in carrying out their plans and goals is limited—even for well-adjusted teens. Communication is the key to success. There are very few, if any, goals that are reached without overcoming challenges and making some compromises.

5. *True.* Listening to the rhythms in music (depending on the music, of course) can help the brain achieve a soothed state of mind.

6. *True.* Adderall, for example, is a stimulant similar to cocaine that can lead to use of more addictive drugs. Anytime you give a pill that numbs emotions to a teenager, you are creating a major problem in that teenager's development.

7. *False.* Venting anger without conflict resolution only builds more anger. A teenager who "vents" will come to feel entitled to express rage without feeling obligated to find more socially acceptable ways of dealing with their anger.

8. *False.* This is a new age, with new issues.

9. *False.* The wants and desires of teenagers never end. There is a big difference between meeting a teenager's *wants*—designer outfits and expensive electronics, for example— and meeting their *needs* in the form of nurturing, structure, and support, as well as providing adequate food, shelter, and clothing. Too often parents learn early how to satisfy a child's wants, yet they remain in the dark as to how to meet their needs.

10. *True.* As odd as it sounds, breathing patterns are contagious, and certain patterns convey assurance while others convey stress. When I worked with the families in

the pediatric oncology ward at Stanford University School of Medicine, I found that if families breathed (and spoke) calmly and deliberately, the children responded better to them and to their treatments.

11. *True.* Drugs are toxic to the body and to the brain. The more recreational drugs a teenager takes, the more vulnerable the brain becomes.

12. *False.* Talking to teenagers about drug abuse when they are high is never productive. Logic and reasoning are compromised, and so is memory. A teenager is not capable of serious discussion or good decisions when stoned.

13. *False.* Your child does not know how to behave without your guidance. You may have taught him or her in younger years, but in the adolescent and teen years, attitudes shift due to hormonal and brain changes. Friends have newfound influence. Parents must set boundaries.

14. *False.* Parents must find more constructive and supportive ways to discourage self-destructive behavior.

15. *False.* Parents must clearly define and enforce boundaries.

Myths of Parenthood Debunked

Children change as they enter adolescence—and so should your parenting. Do not hold on to the myths of parenting! Those myths (and the contrasting realities) include the following:

1. "I believe that my child loves me because I am the parent and I have always loved my child."

    Reality check: Your children may respect you for being their parent, but an addict's craving for drugs overpowers all else—including the bonds between parent and child.

2. "My parents were very tough on me, and I am who I am today *because* they were tough. I will be tough on my children and they will resent it now but love me for it later."

    Reality check: You are who you are today because of *you*. Your parents paid attention to you and provided you with guidelines—but you made your own choices.

3. "I am going to give my children everything I didn't have—and they will love me for it."

    Reality check: The question is: *If you give them everything, what will be left for them to earn?*

4. "I am going to tell my children I love them every day so they will understand unconditional love."

     Reality check: Unconditional love is not what you tell them—it is what you show them.

5. "My children know that I love them because I pay for everything."

     Reality check: Paying for everything is a good way to teach children to be irresponsible.

6. "Guilt is a good way to keep children in line."

     Reality check: Guilt builds resentment and fear, not respect or self-control.

7. "My children owe me, so they will make good grades and perform well in sports and activities."

     Reality check: Your children may one day realize they are in your debt, but in the teen years, they will tend to feel that they are entitled—which can become a problem if they are drawn to drugs.

Requirements for Addiction Recovery

Now that we've debunked some parenting myths, let's take a look at what is truly required on the part of parents and teens on the path to recovery.

REQUIRED: A Belief in Some Form of Benevolent Power

I believe an addict needs to believe in a loving, benevolent higher power in order to overcome an addiction to drugs or alcohol. An addict should make a conscious decision to trust the "power of love" beyond the common use of the term. This may feel mystical or religious, because it acknowledges a transformative force beyond personal egos and human powers, but I believe it is an important aspect of an addict's recovery.

The term *transformative* relates to a transition to a high level of existence and self-understanding. To heal and move forward, the addict, as well as the family members, should take transformative steps that require tapping into a higher power for deliverance. To reach and accept new goals that don't include drug abuse, an addict and his or her support team need a time and place for renewal. The spiritual realm offers opportunities both for renewal and forgiveness.

REQUIRED: Natural Healing Skills

Many of the tools used to deal with addiction have been around for as long as addiction has existed. I believe that "natural" treatments can heal addictions. Modern drugs, even methadone, have their place, but in many cases, we can also learn from and use certain proven ancient techniques.

I first studied the techniques of Native American shamans early in my training as a dolorologist (a doctor concerned with the study and treatment of pain), while

I worked as a clinical professor of orthopedic surgery at University of Texas Southwestern Medical Center. My quest was to study what the shaman did for pain, since some of the chronic patients I was trying to help were not responding well to conventional medication. In this exploration of ancient treatments, I was introduced to the spiritual leader of the Taos Pueblo, who in turn introduced me to his wife. She showed me her healing technique based on massage. She explained her belief that we get sick when our "mental energies" get caught up in the body's tissue masses. Her technique was one of freeing those energies through intensive muscle massage. I found it fascinating that she said this treatment was also used to cure addiction.

She used no specific type of massage for drug addiction; instead, her methods addressed the *cause* of addiction by targeting certain areas of the body. Although I can cite no scientific basis to prove why this method works, I've achieved positive results with it myself, and I've heard of others who have had similar experiences.

Potential Cause of Addiction	Area to Be Massaged
Loss of self-esteem	Chest
Drug toxicity	Lower belly and feet
Confusion	Shoulders
Anger	Jaw muscles
Guilt	Eyes

Richard Pavak, head of The Shen Therapy Institute in Sausalito, California, also uses touch techniques successfully in treating addiction. As a trained engineer, he believes that the body is made up of energy circuitry. He feels that disease, especially mental disease, is the result of these "circuits" becoming backed up. (For more information on Shen Therapy, visit www.shentherapy.info.)

REQUIRED: Empathy

Empathy, the ability to relate emotionally and compassionately to others, is a critical part of communication. Showing empathy is the first step in communication—and it may be the most important form of communicating with your teenager. Yet simply saying "I understand" is not enough. Here are the three basic levels of empathetic responses:

- **Level I:** You reflect feelings back to your teenager.
- **Level II:** You reflect feelings with some background related to your experience.
- **Level III:** You reflect feeling and add some cause and effect.

For example, assume that your teenager tells you she stole some money from you to pay for drugs and that she is now sorry. A Level I response might be, "I can understand how desperate you must have been and that you want forgiveness now." This is direct expression of the feeling without saying much more.

A Level II response might be, "You must have been desperate, and I can remember when I was so scared I might have done something like that once." This response includes reflection with your own related personal story to show you've been in a similar situation.

A Level III response might be, "You must have been so desperate and needy you didn't care where you got the money. You were even willing to break your own principles and steal from a family member." This response includes shared feelings, experiences, and an understanding of underlying issues.

Human experience varies greatly, but we generally share a common language for expressing our feelings. If teenagers are having a difficult time expressing themselves, communication will suffer. However, there are ways parents can help a child better communicate. The following is a list of terms that cover a wide range of emotions. Give this list to your child and encourage your teenager to use this list when trying to express how he or she feels:

- Afraid
- Angry
- Anxious
- Ashamed
- Bored
- Confused
- Contemptuous
- Depressed
- Disgusted
- Distressed

- Enraged
- Excited
- Exhausted
- Frightened
- Guilty
- Lonely
- Overwhelmed
- Sad
- Shy
- Suspicious

To help families at my clinic, we have an artist draw the faces of children displaying a range of emotions. We then ask the families to place the pictures on their refrigerators with different magnets for each member of the family. Every night, each family member places a magnet on the picture of the facial expression that best captures how he or she feels, and then explains why he or she feels that way. This exercise helps children learn what they are feeling and how to better express their emotions.

Empathy statements are also helpful in demonstrating to teenagers that parents understand their feelings. Empathy simply requires that you demonstrate an understanding of how someone else is feeling without judgment or without trying to solve the problem. This can be difficult for a concerned parent. You don't have to worry about developing the perfect response, or even about being correct in your assessment of the child's emotional state. Once lines of communication are open, teenagers will let you know how they feel. Here is an example of how an empathetic interaction should go:

> **Child:** "I am really mad at you. You don't seem to trust me, and you are watching my every move. I want you to stop it."
>
> **Response:** "First, let me see if I hear you right. You are telling me how angry you are, that you are about to blow your top, and the reason is that I am spying on you. Is that right?"
>
> **Child:** "Yes, you are always asking me questions about my friends, my schoolwork—everything!"
>
> **Response:** "I must be irritating you a lot lately."
>
> **Child:** "Yes, and I need some privacy. I need time to do what I do without you poking your head into my business."
>
> **Response:** "I get your point about being irritated and the emotional heat it brings up. It seems to come up often lately. What do you think is going on?"

In this way, you can open the doors to communication. To keep these doors open between you and your teenager, continue to demonstrate a desire to understand feelings before trying to judge or fix behavior.

I'm advising you to focus on feelings and emotions as a way to establish rapport without confrontation. We all view the world from a unique perspective informed by our experiences. Parents and children are no different. You may not know what your child has experienced, but you likely have shared similar feelings and emotions. You can communicate based on shared emotional experience even when your child feels that you will never understand what it is like to be in the same situation.

REQUIRED: Unconditional Regard

The primary force for reaching an addicted child is love in action, which can be defined for our purposes as "unconditional regard." Unlike empathy, unconditional regard is communicated mostly in nonverbal ways. The way you look at your child can demonstrate compassion and support. If you don't look at your child during conversations, it might convey disinterest. When dealing with an addicted child, focus on the conversation and put aside the cell phone or other distractions.

On the other hand, don't stare at your child or look at him or her with suspicion—even when you *are* suspicious. Any evidence of distrust cuts off communication faster than pressing the "end" button on your cell phone. To keep discussions going, especially when emotions are running high, train yourself to be attentive, focused on your child's emotions, nonjudgmental, and more intent on understanding than "fixing."

Body language speaks louder than words. Do you turn your body away from your child when discussing a problem? Do you clench your fists? Do you breathe irregularly? Do you talk quickly and act jittery? Do you talk too loudly or too softly? Do the muscles in your neck, back, or jaws get tight and tense? These are all cues that your child can pick up on, and they may trigger a defensive attitude. Your child knows your body language; he or she has studied it since birth! Pay attention to your body language. Make sure it reflects your receptive and caring spirit.

Forgiveness is another important tool for reaching your addicted child. This does not mean you must condone self-destructive behavior. It is not about forgetting the past or acting as though it never happened. Nor does forgiveness mean that there are not consequences for past actions that merit disciplinary actions.

Forgiveness is the release of emotional attachment associated with an event. Your addicted child might have stolen money, which would understandably be of concern. But once that has been discussed and consequences have been set, there is no need to bring it up again. Parents often make the mistake of bringing up past offenses, which constitutes repeat punishment for the child. In a court of law, you can't be tried twice for the same crime. The same should hold true in parenting.

Forgiveness means letting go of the past. You can remember the past without emotional attachment. Of course, if your child steals again, you can and should bring up the previous offense to make the point that the consequences will be more severe because the bad behavior has continued.

REQUIRED: **Genuineness**

While empathy involves expressing your under-standing of your child's feelings without judgment, gen-uineness is about expressing your own feelings honestly. You should share how *you* feel about the situation, but without casting blame. Take responsibility for your own reactions. Examples of non-genuine statements include:

- "You made me lose my job!"
- "You made me lose my temper!"
- "You made me wreck my car!"
- "You made me miss my appointment!"
- "You ruined my golf game!"
- "You are my biggest worry."
- "You drive me crazy."
- "If you weren't around, I would have a good life."
- "You give me headaches!"
- "You give me ulcers!"
- "You are the cause of this family's problems."

Examples of genuine responses include:

- "I feel pretty lost right now. I don't know what to do."

- "I'm worried about you and what you are going through."

- "I hope for better days, but I think we will both learn from going through this stressful time together."

- "I realize that you get pretty mad at me and think I am dumb, but I will always love you and I hope for the best for you."

- "I wish that I could express to you in a way you would understand how committed I am to making your life the best it can possibly be."

Genuineness is more difficult than the other two communication requirements (unconditional regard and empathy) because it asks the parent to act as a model of honesty. Genuineness requires that you articulate your emotions, as well as what has triggered them, to help someone who may be hostile to you gain a better understanding of your relationship.

Sometimes it helps to put things in perspective by citing your own experiences. An example of this would be to say, "My father always told me to do what is right because you have to live with yourself. If you cheat, you will never be proud of your accomplishment. You know what? He was right."

Make a Plan

When I was about 15 years old, my parents took me aside and explained that as I was growing into manhood, I would make mistakes along the way. They were right, of course, but I did learn from my mistakes. The challenge in life is not to make the sort of mistakes that can cause a lifetime of regret. For that reason, my parents prepared me by listing the mistakes I would likely make and challenges I would encounter before the age of 21. Then they explained how they would deal with those mistakes if they did occur. The list of probable mistakes and challenges they gave me included:

1. A girl would break my heart.

2. I would have a car wreck.

3. I would get in trouble with the law simply for being in the wrong place at the wrong time.

4. I would experiment with smoking and drinking.

5. I would estimate my parents' IQs to be lower than needed for raising a teenager, and consequently I would think about running away.

6. I would have my first true love (which meant sex, but I didn't catch on to that until later).

7. I would have a fistfight.

They were mostly right about numbers 1, 2, 4, 5, and 6. I can't express how shocked I was that my behavior was so predictable, or how relieved I was when I realized my parents had it covered in terms of their responses. I always knew that my family would be there for me, even though I also realized there would be consequences to pay for the mistakes I made. (I did get in trouble with the law and I did have a fistfight, but I talked my way out of serious trouble. I had a gift for problem solving—thanks to my parents!)

✦ ✦

Teenagers need guidance on how to manage stress and how to deal with difficult situations. They don't know what they don't know, even though they often seem to think they have all the answers. Their brains are still developing and their hormones are raging, so be gentle. Teenagers can be confused by all of the changes they are undergoing physically and emotionally. Help them learn life skills early on. Keep lines of communication open, even when the topics seem trivial. These open lines will be more important when life gets more serious and the challenges grow from dealing with pimples and homework to the stress of facing peer pressure to use drugs or watch pornography.

Today's teenagers need every resource available because of the intense pressures they face. Help your children develop emotional intelligence so they can discern who is trustworthy and who is not—and so they know what they need to do to win the trust of others. Teach your child to reach out to others in need, and to put into relationships as much as, or more than, they take out.

✦ ✦ ✦

CHAPTER TEN

INTENTION AND PRAYER FOR DEALING WITH TEENAGE ADDICTION IN A FAMILY

When a family comes to me in an addiction crisis, I seek every conceivable path to peace and resolution. One of the paths I suggest is that of intention and prayer, because I believe you can achieve results from both science and faith. This chapter borrows from Larry Dossey, M.D., and his many books on prayer and medicine, including *Be Careful What You Pray For . . . You Just Might Get It* (1998), *Prayer Is Good Medicine* (1997), *Healing Words* (1995), and *Recovering the Soul* (1989), as well as *The Energy of Prayer* (2006), a book by Thich Nhat Hanh for which Dr. Dossey wrote the Introduction.

Dr. Dossey is an accomplished and well-respected scientist who has conducted more than 160 verifiable studies on how human consciousness influences the healing process. He gives clear explanations without prejudice or reference to religious views, and his research is conducted with the highest standards. Like Dr. Dossey, I will discuss intention and prayer from a nondenominational basis without reference to any specific religious bias. Prayer is primarily a way to connect with a Supreme Being while encouraging devotion and discipline to principles. It need not involve dogma of any kind.

Intention

The key to success with prayer is intention—which includes both direction and purpose. Projecting intention is as old as humankind. While some cultures are known for practicing hexes, the negative form of projecting intention, there are plenty of examples of spiritual figures who practice helpful magic and healing spells.

For example, in 1998, forest fires raged in the Amazonian state of Roraima and destroyed a tremendous wealth of rain forest. The whole region was in severe drought, and for almost a quarter of the year, not a single drop of water fell upon the hot, humid, and dying land. In the late spring, two shamans of the indigenous Yanomami tribe were called in to see if they could do something to bring the blessed rain. As they danced and prayed to their spirits, they appeared to rise above the anxieties and depression of their distressed people. The shamans looked confident and unafraid as they expressed their spiritual beliefs without fear of condemnation or criticism. After the second day, the rains came and restored balance to the region, extinguishing the previously uncontrollable fire and encouraging new vegetation and growth.

Examples of such events where people effect miracles that transform a person or a situation come from all over the world. And only with honest, objective reporting of such events could one believe in the potential of spiritual transformation—the transformation of your purpose in life. This has applications, I believe, in healing addiction, which requires transforming nearly every aspect of the addict's life.

Science supports these reports in definable ways with experiments in which conditions can be controlled and natural distractions limited. Nothing can be absolutely controlled, of course, but the results of these studies can nevertheless be extremely enlightening.

Here's an interesting example: We've done fascinating experiments in which we separate two people, putting them in different parts of a building, and then have one send positive thoughts to the other while we monitor brain activity. We found that the physiology of the person receiving the positive thoughts was altered and levels of stress were reduced. I have also read studies in which identical twins were found to communicate or "feel" each other's emotions despite being separated by great distances.

Perhaps we do not need scientific studies to tell us that we have the capacity to help or hurt others, but we do have a call to love and serve each other. We are the keepers of our brothers and sisters, and getting support from one's family can be extremely important and powerful in helping a teenage addict to heal.

Powering Up Intention

According to the research literature, the most powerful state of consciousness for prayer is a relaxed state of high concentration. This has been called the *alpha* or *theta* brain-wave state. If you enter into these states, you feel very calm and cannot easily be distracted. Your breath is easier and slower than normal, and your mind is not stressed. You feel content to listen, and experience your pleasurable but not sleepy state. Your mind is open to the sounds of heaven or God's words.

The power of this state increases if an entire group of people reaches it together. This mutual state of consciousness can be achieved in several ways. The most common is to sing together or merely hum the same note. The vibration supports group members in rising to a higher level of consciousness.

Focusing on breathing patterns is also a popular method of reaching higher levels of consciousness, both individually and in a group. These intentions can be guided by the voice of a leader, who may give the group special directions to follow, such as staying strong against evil forces or feeling love for others or for God.

Compassion and Love Are Most Powerful

Although this discussion may be intellectual, the power of connection comes through love. Lead your intention through your heart as well as your mind. Visualize the blessings or influences coming to your addicted teenager in the form of symbols, colors, or animal imagery. This works because the mind understands symbols. Imagine that your intention has a positive influence at a spiritual level. Know that your intentions are received and answered.

At some point you will allow the intention to be carried beyond your individual self or group, and beyond the exact images you see or feel, into another reality.

"Let go and let God" is a phrase often heard in prayers (and also in AA). You will experience the peace of knowing that your intentions are heard. Don't be limited by your vision of the physical world.

The Segments of Prayer

Prayer can be defined as the process through which a person of faith calls upon a higher spiritual power. Prayers can carry any sort of message or request, including a parent's plea for help in healing an addicted child. I have observed the powerful effects of prayer in the lives of teenage addicts, and I have seen critical positive changes in the families who use prayer. Some of these changes within the families are difficult for them to describe other than as "deep feelings of warmth and love," but hope and faith are definitely enhanced by prayer.

Parents explain to me that prayer has kept the doors open to healing possibilities not only in their children's lives but also in their other relationships. It is very easy for family members to blame each other, especially when the teenager is blaming everyone for the addiction. Being a parent can be a blessing, but the trauma and conflict of an addicted child can be hellish. Prayer appears to enhance mutual respect between an addict and loved ones, which invites healing. One of the reasons why I think the 12-step program works is that it opens the addict to the possibilities of feeling special and loved by others. The potential for being forgiven for past mistakes is introduced, which allows for transformation and renewal. Prayer has a similar effect. It brings in a higher power who loves the individual unconditionally, one who has a purpose in mind for us all.

Hope cannot be underestimated as a factor in rehabilitation of a teenager and his or her family. Even though the teenager may be behaving in a very destructive manner, addicts know they are out of control. In their hearts, most want to regain control of their lives and their thoughts.

In years past, I have experimented with the power of extended love in treating addicted teenagers. I have formed groups and taught them to project feelings of love and well-being to a selected individual during a one-hour session. Then I've taken the individual into another room and, using sensitive biofeedback equipment, measured skin temperature, muscle tension, and skin conductivity as I had the group focus on projecting the feelings of love and well-being toward the person. The group sent positive thoughts and imagined their own body temperatures rising as a sign of relaxation and healing. We did this for five minutes and then rested five minutes. Concurrently, I measured the subject's body temperature and relaxation levels.

The measures correlated directly with the activities of the group—except the change in readings came approximately 30 seconds before the group projected their feelings of love. I also found that the entire group experienced elevated levels of self-esteem and warmth toward each other during this experiment. This is common in Dr. Dossey's work as well.

Prayer clearly elevates hopeful feelings, emotional strength, and the faith of addicted teenagers and their families. Prayer invites new opportunities and increases optimism. Prayer keeps the addict and loved ones from despairing and opens the door for greater wisdom and understanding.

How Do You Pray?

Prayer is practiced in many ways, and how one prays is a very personal choice. However, there are models and parts to prayer that pertain to all common forms. To a greater or lesser extent, prayer can be broken down into seven segments, and any one segment can be a prayer in itself. With no intention to limit this concept of prayer to Christians, I will use the Lord's Prayer, as practiced in many churches, as an example of the different segments.

Segment 1:
Recognition of Supreme Authority

Our Father, which art in Heaven,
Hallowed be thy name;
Thy kingdom come;
Thy will be done
On Earth as it is in Heaven.

These phrases, brief as they are, acknowledge that the Supreme Being is *the* authority. This higher being has dominion over all earthly matters, and we as humans lack the glorious wisdom and power that is beyond our knowledge and understanding.

As we acknowledge the Supreme Being, we are in turn acknowledged. It means we have faith in that which we cannot see. The voices of our egos are silenced when we accept that there is a power greater than ourselves.

This segment in itself defines prayer because it offers perspective on the human condition. It opens us up to the possibility of miracles and a higher power who is behind a plan for our lives over which we have no control. By expressing the concept of "let go and let God" and "not my will, but thy will," we admit that the higher power has control of our lives.

This prayer segment is especially relevant to the first step in the 12-step program because it acknowledges that the addict or alcoholic needs help on a spiritual level. The addict can benefit from certain actions and from the assistance of others, but this prayer acknowledges that spiritual insight and faith also play a critical role in the healing process.

SEGMENT 2:
Request for Sustenance

Give us this day our daily bread.

This segment is a modest request for help. In these terms, sustenance refers to the nurturing we need to be of service. In this, we are asking the higher power to help the addict and the family overcome the destructive power of drugs and alcohol and to heal the damage done. According to Dr. Dossey, there are two types of requests for assistance: *direct* and *open-ended*. Direct requests are generally for specific outcomes, such as more peace, an end to drinking alcohol or drug abuse, or a more stable life. The open-ended requests are more akin to "thy will be done," which is a request for the higher spiritual power to do what it deems best to serve the higher good.

Most of Dr. Dossey's studies show that maximum benefits are derived from open-ended prayers. In truth, we don't have the capacity to understand what constitutes the ultimate good or the highest purpose for our lives or the lives of others. Most people of faith believe that only the highest spiritual power knows what is best.

Consider the case of Sadie, a 14-year-old prostitute and severe heroin addict. She rejected her family, instead offering her body to strangers in exchange for drugs. She was hostile and bitter. She had sex with multiple partners without telling them she had HIV and hepatitis, which is a criminal offense. She'd become both physically and mentally ill.

I believe that prayer led to her rehabilitation. Eventually, Sadie graduated from law school. She now does legal work for many battered women. Her proud mother told me that she never gave up on Sadie. She prayed that her daughter would one day serve God in some way, even if she died from her addiction. Sadie's mother now believes that it was necessary for Sadie to go through addiction to find the path God intended for her. Through her addiction, she attained in-depth wisdom and insights into other women in need. It goes without saying that family prayers helped advance peace and understanding in the treatment of Sadie's addiction. Prayer does make a difference, but it may not always be in the way we expect.

Segment 3:
Reciprocity of Action

And forgive us our trespasses
As we forgive those who trespass against us.

In this segment, the prayer commits to a higher form of living. Instead of the anger and resentment of victimization, this calls for forgiveness on a spiritual level. Prayers can change behavior patterns and put us more in alignment with God's plan.

This segment is unique in that it asks the Supreme Being to join us in practicing forgiveness so that the individual "pays forward" by forgiving another. This applies to addicts forgiving themselves as well as those who they believe may have enabled or encouraged their addictive behavior—and it applies to the families of addicts who must forgive hurts and damage done during the addiction. Forgiveness is essential to healing for all parties.

Segment 4:
Request for Guidance

And lead us not into temptation.

This segment implies that as human beings, we are not perfect and our lack of wisdom can make us act out of egotism. Pride, lust, wrath, greed, sloth, envy, and gluttony (the famous "seven deadly sins") are all human faults. In this prayer, such imperfections are acknowledged, and guidance is requested to maintain a spiritual perspective.

This segment is especially relevant to addiction because of the failings of addicts. The disease of addiction undermines a belief in principles and values. Addicts have no moral compass. They lose track of lessons they've learned and those that are ingrained in us all regarding how to treat other people.

No one is immune to human failings and poor judgment. Sometimes, I think our flaws are meant to keep us humble. One of my temptations is arrogance, especially if I have just been honored in some way. I was once on an airplane headed home from a *Dr. Phil* taping in which many people had thanked me for my contributions to a show. I noticed that many of the elderly people boarding the plane appeared to be confused about their seat assignments. They seemed anxious and in need of assistance.

Then I heard someone say, "Excuse me, sir, but I think you are in my seat." It turned out to be a very elderly man who was speaking to me. Initially, I judged him as being one of the confused older folks, since I clearly thought I was in my assigned seat. But as it turned out, *I* was the confused person. He was right. I'd plunked down in the wrong seat—his seat. I had to laugh at my somewhat arrogant assumptions about who was confused and who needed help—and at my own folly.

SEGMENT 5:
An Awareness of Evil Intentions

But deliver us from evil.

This segment is controversial in that it acknowledges that evil exists in our world. The evil within men and women stems from sick minds who want to hurt or defeat others by any means. Those like Adolf Hitler, who use their power to enslave others, destroy hope and love, and wreak destruction are also "evil" by this definition. I believe the dark force of evil exists, but I also believe that goodness can help us avoid it and even defeat it.

My late friend Patricia was a prayer therapist and an amazing woman who had a tremendous faith in God. For example, if she thought God was telling her to go to Israel, she'd somehow find the right people and resources to help her get there. When she prayed for others, she could help dissolve their anger and guilt. This worked very well with addicts because they had so much anger directed both inwardly and outwardly. By relieving these extremely destructive or "evil" thoughts, Patricia helped them get rid of their reasons for abusing drugs or alcohol. For example, I'd worked with people who had severe hostility toward their parents because of their addictions, but when prayer was introduced, they began seeing their parents on a more spiritual level, relieving their anxiety and anger toward them.

I was amazed by Patricia's intelligence and the validated results she produced. I studied her work as part of my scientific efforts to understand the power of prayer. I recommended a number of patients to her, including addicted teenagers, and these prayer sessions were very effective in shaping these patients' destinies. I concluded that prayer absolutely has the potential to banish evil and bring about insight within a sphere of deep and open consciousness.

SEGMENT 6:
Thanksgiving

For thine is the kingdom
And the power
And the glory,
Forever.

In a full circle, the prayer is brought back to recognition of a higher power that we as limited beings can only imagine. In psychological experiments, this segment is usually regarded as the mystery of consciousness or the "mind projection field." The main point is the acknowledgment of that enduring power, its importance in our lives, and the need to show our gratitude for it in the way we live and pray.

SEGMENT 7:
Conclusion and Affirmation

Amen.

One of the most important segments in prayer is its final affirmation of all that was said or expressed in the prayer. The word *amen* is a transliteration of a Hebrew word that means *so be it* or *surely*. The Hebrew root word from which it is drawn means to be faithful or trustworthy. An extension of the word has been given as "I believe."

Amen is not the only word for conclusion of prayer. In the Muslin tradition, the ending term is *amin*, coming from the same derivation and meaning. In many Native American prayers, the word *ho* is used the same way.

We may not put much emphasis on *amen* in our prayers, but it has been shown to be an important aspect of prayer, a final confirmation and affirmation of belief. Our beliefs determine our actions, so the *amen* has power in guiding us to live according to our faith. When an addict prays and confirms spiritual beliefs, it helps that individual in the fight to overcome and heal from addiction.

The Power of Prayer

We have different dimensions in our lives. We have the physical dimension of our bodies, the psychological dimension of how and why we live the way we do, and finally the spiritual dimension. Each dimension has certain cause-and-effect laws from which we learn and become wiser. To an extent, these dimensions define our whole lives. We know very little about the spiritual dimension because our minds are limited. I don't profess to know all the laws and principles that make our spirituality so critical, but nevertheless it is the primary reason humans are unique in the animal kingdom.

The spiritual dimension is one in which we evolve and transform. We can improve through education and insights, but these improvements are limited to our personal lives. The spiritual processes of evolution have included rituals and ceremonies used to enhance our feeling of connection to a higher power or Supreme Being from humanity's earliest days. We cannot deny the beneficial effects. This is the way we can evolve our souls for purposes beyond our own physical and psychological lives. The spiritual realm offers us hope for ourselves, for our children, for our families, and for the entire world. Through the spiritual, we aspire to a purpose greater than ourselves.

By definition, an addicted person is paralyzed physiologically, psychologically, and spiritually. Just because the addict attains sobriety doesn't mean the individual has escaped the prison of the addiction. Spirituality is the only door to lasting recovery, because it offers a greater purpose and a higher experience.

✦ ✦ ✦

AFTERWORD

Saving Your Child

This book was born of a passion for assisting addicted teenagers and their families. I hope the material has been helpful, enlightening, and of practical use. The epidemic of teenage addiction and drug and alcohol abuse is truly tragic. Because teenagers' brains are at such a critical developmental stage, substance abuse can effectively paralyze the brain's protective forces, leaving these young people incredibly vulnerable and at risk for permanent and irreversible damage physically, emotionally, and intellectually.

Adolescence is a monumental phase in life, full of promise and joy—as well as danger. Teenagers generally lack the ability to assess risk or to see the long-term consequences of their actions. They are also just beginning to figure out how they fit into society and what their value will be. It's never an easy period, for the teenagers or for their parents!

Most parents want to protect their children, but their ability to do so becomes more and more difficult as a teenager pushes for independence. Often, the only option is for the parent to step back and take on the roles of coach, cheerleader, and, whenever possible, gentle guide.

How do parents accept those roles? It's estimated that people remember only 10 percent of what they hear and 30 percent of what they read, but they remember about 80 percent of what they see and do. The vast majority of actual learning comes through personal experience.

Parents cannot judge themselves by the mistakes their children make. They should give teenagers room to figure out things for themselves—as long as they are not endangering themselves or others. The best parents can do, in most cases, is to be available to guide and teach when teaching moments arise. The fact that you are reading this book shows your dedication and love for your children, yourself, and your family.

Challenges, setbacks, and obstacles are a natural part of growing up and living in this world. Our children will likely experience heartbreak, loneliness, criticism, judgment, and dishonesty no matter what we try to do to shelter and forewarn them. They will likely lie to us, disappoint us, and defy us at some point. Remember, we have all gone through our teenage years, and most of us survive without serious damage. Teenagers who at risk for drug and alcohol abuse or become addicted require special attention and possible intervention through treatment, tough love, and professional counseling. But with an action plan founded on unconditional love, compassion, and empathy for the teenager's feelings and perspective, parents can guide them through even these most considerable challenges. I've written this book to give you the benefit of my experiences working with thousands of young people and their families.

✦ ✦

An even more complex and possibly dangerous future lies ahead, but we have the advantage of experience and education. I encourage you to work through the barriers to interpersonal communication posed by smartphones, texting, and e-mail. Take every opportunity for one-on-one time, walks, meals, and outings, so that you know your child and your child knows and trusts you. It is so important to share spiritual beliefs, to worship and to pray together, and to establish what is right and wrong through time-honored moral principles and values. It is perhaps most critical to the health of your relationship with your children that you talk about the small things—so that when big things come up, the lines are open and clear.

Talking about the dangers of drugs and alcohol before your child hits the teenage years reduces the chance that a teenager will abuse substances or become addicted. If your child already has been abusing drugs and alcohol, the time to plan for an early intervention is sooner rather than later. You don't want your child to fall into a rapid downward spiral that cannot be stopped. In my opinion, parents spend far too much time these days preparing their children for a career in sports or entertainment or other possibly high-paying professions and not enough time preparing them to communicate their feelings; take responsibility for their actions and their happiness; resolve personal problems without self-medicating; and navigate life with emotional intelligence, empathy, and compassion for others.

I do encourage parents to introduce their children to sports and to support them in anything that helps them become stronger physically and disciplined mentally. There are healthy aspects to competitive sports, but too often winning a prize is emphasized over teamwork and personal improvement. If the teenager's goal is always to do their best by improving and learning every day, then even mistakes, failures, and setbacks become part of the bigger process of continual growth.

Participating in track and football as a teenager had a major and lasting impact on my life. I probably ranked 27th on our 27-member football squad when I joined the team, but I grew to be good enough to play at the college level. My growth as a player gave me great confidence and a deep appreciation for the value of team effort. Track, on the other hand, taught me self-reliance and self-discipline, which was perhaps an even greater gift. I learned that the only comparison I needed to make was to myself. I learned to run faster, to focus on continual improvement, and to celebrate my achievements every step of the way.

These are things we should help our children to discover, either through competitive sports or other character-building, fitness-enhancing experiences. We can be friends to our children when they are mature adults. When they are teenagers, they need us to guide them, coach them, protect them, and prepare them.

Being a parent of a teenager is a tough job. If you are intimidated by the challenges facing you, welcome to the club. You are not alone. It's rare for a parent not to have fears and doubts, but you should know there is plenty of help available. (In Appendix C, you'll find a list of recovery resources you can call upon.) Focus on doing your best for the child as a role model, teacher, coach, and spiritual guide. Every teenager rebels at some point. It's part of the process of growing up. Of course, the teenager who abuses drugs and alcohol presents challenges above and beyond the norm. Your biggest trials will come with the lies and betrayal of trust. Keep in mind that it is not the teenager but the disease afflicting the teenager's mind and body.

Do not lose hope. I have seen love overcome the demons of addiction again and again. I know the pain of having an addicted teenager disrupt the family, but I also know the joy of seeing the child emerge from the disease with a rare wisdom and depth of understanding that comes with surviving such a difficult journey. The rewards of standing up and fighting for your child will be reaped over two lifetimes—yours and that of the wonderful adult you've helped save from the horrible fate of addiction.

✦ ✦ ✦

BIBLIOGRAPHY

ADAA. (2007). 2007 Stress & Anxiety Disorders Study. *Anxiety Disorders of America*.

Aftanas, L., & Golosheykin, S. (2005). Impact of regular meditation practice on EEG activity at rest and during evoked negative emotions. *Int J Neurosci, 115*(6), 893–909.

Biederman, J., Wilens, T., Mick, E., Milberger, S., Spencer, T. J., & Faraone, S. V. (1995). Psychoactive substance use disorders in adults with attention deficit hyperactivity disorder (ADHD): effects of ADHD and psychiatric comorbidity. *Am J Psychiatry, 152*(11), 1652–1665.

Bittman, B., Berk, L., Shannon, M., Sharaf, M., Westengard, J., Guegler, K. J., et al. (2005). Recreational music-making modulates the human stress response: a preliminary individualized gene expression strategy. *Med Sci Monit, 11*(2), BR31–40.

Buzsaki, G. (2006). *Rhythms of the Brain*. Oxford: Oxford University Press.

Carmody, J., & Baer, R. A. (2008). Relationships between mindfulness practice and levels of mindfulness, medical and psychological symptoms and well-being in a mindfulness-based stress reduction program. *J Behav Med. 31*(1), 23–33.

Cartwright, D. (2002). The narcissistic exoskeleton: the defensive organization of the rage-type murderer. *Bull Menninger Clin, 66*(1), 1–18.

Chapell, M. S. (1994). Inner speech and respiration: toward a possible mechanism of stress reduction. *Percept Mot Skills, 79*(2), 803–811.

Dossey, L. (2009). *The Power of Premonitions: How Knowing the Future Can Shape Our Lives*. New York: Dutton.

———. (2006). *The Extraordinary Healing Power of Ordinary Things.* New York: Harmony/Random House.

———. (2001). *Healing Beyond the Body.* Boston: Shambhala.

———. (1999). *Reinventing Medicine.* San Francisco: HarperSanFrancisco.

———. (1997). *Be Careful What You Pray For.* San Francisco: HarperSanFrancisco.

———. (1996). *Prayer Is Good Medicine.* San Francisco: HarperSanFrancisco.

———. (1993). *Healing Words: The Power of Prayer in the Practice of Medicine.* San Francisco: HarperSanFrancisco.

———. (1989). *Recovering the Soul.* New York: Bantam.

———. (1984). *Beyond Illness.* Boston: New Science Library.

Esch, T., Duckstein, J., Welke, J., & Braun, V. (2007). Mind/body techniques for physiological and psychological stress reduction: Stress management via Tai Chi training—a pilot study. *Med Sci Monit, 13*(11), CR488–497.

Floresco, S. B., & Ghods-Sharifi, S. (2007). Amygdala-prefrontal cortical circuitry regulates effort-based decision making. *Cereb. Cortex, 17*(2), 251–260.

Flory, K., Molina, B. S., Pelham, W. E., Jr., Gnagy, E., & Smith, B. (2006). Childhood ADHD predicts risky sexual behavior in young adulthood. *J Clin Child Adolesc Psychol, 35*(4), 571–577.

Foote, B., Smolin, Y., Neft, D. I., & Lipschitz, D. (2008). Dissociative disorders and suicidality in psychiatric outpatients. *J Nerv Ment Dis, 196*(1), 29–36.

Freeman, L., & Lawlis, F. *Mosby's Complementary and Alternative Medicine* (2001). St. Louis: Mosby.

Gordon, S. M., Tulak, F., & Troncale, J. (2004). Prevalence and characteristics of adolescents patients with co-occurring ADHD and substance dependence. *J Addict Dis, 23*(4), 31–40.

Jones S., Bonci A. (2005). Synaptic plasticity and drug addiction. *Curr Opin Pharmacol, 5*(1), 20–25.

Kalivas, P. W., Volkow, N. D. (2005). The neural basis of addiction: a pathology of motivation and choice. *Am J Psychiatry, 162*(8), 1403–1413.

Kjellgren, A., Bood, S. A., Axelsson, K., Norlander, T., & Saatcioglu, F. (2007). Wellness through a comprehensive Yogic breathing program—A controlled pilot trial. *BMC Complement Altern Med, 7*(1), 43.

Klassen, A. F., Miller, A., & Fine, S. (2004). Health-related quality of life in children and adolescents who have a diagnosis of attention-deficit/hyperactivity disorder. *Pediatrics, 114*(5), e541–547.

Kourrich, S., Rothwell, P. E, Klug, J. R., Thomas, M. J. (2007). Cocaine experience controls bidirectional synaptic plasticity in the nucleus accumbens. *J. Neurosci, 27*(30), 7921–7928.

Krauss, M. R., Russell, R. K., Powers, T. E., & Li, Y. (2006). Accession standards for attention-deficit/hyperactivity disorder: a survival analysis of military recruits, 1995–2000. *Mil Med, 171*(2), 99–102.

Labbe, E., Schmidt, N., Babin, J., & Pharr, M. (2007). Coping with stress: the effectiveness of different types of music. *Appl Psychophysiol Biofeedback, 32*(3–4), 163–168.

LaChance, A. (2006). *Cultural Addiction: The Greenspirit Guide to Recovery.* Berkeley, CA: North Atlantic Books.

Laporte, L., & Guttman, H. (2001). Abusive relationships in families of women with borderline personality disorder, anorexia nervosa and a control group. *J Nerv Ment Dis, 189*(8), 522–531.

Lawlis, F. (2008) *Mending the Broken Bond.* New York: Penguin Group.

———. (2008). *The Stress Answer.* New York: Viking.

———. (2006). *The IQ Answer.* New York: Viking.

———. (2004). *The ADD Answer.* New York: Plume.

———. (1996). *Transpersonal Medicine.* Boston: Shambhala.

Levitin, D. (2007). *This Is Your Brain on Music.* New York: Penguin Group.

Lutz, A., Greischar, L. L., Rawlings, N. B., Ricard, M., & Davidson, R. J. (2004). Long-term meditators self-induce high-amplitude gamma synchrony during mental practice. *Proc Natl Acad Sci U.S.A., 101*(46), 16369–16373.

McTaggart, L. (2007). *The Intention Experiment.* New York: Free Press.

Retz, W., Retz-Junginger, P., Schneider, M., Scherk, H., Hengesch, G., & Rosler, M. (2007). Drug addiction in young prison inmates with and without attention deficit hyperactivity disorder (ADHD). *Fortschr Neurol Psychiatr, 75*(5), 285–292.

Sherman, C. (2007). The defining features of drug intoxication and addiction can be traced to disruptions in cell-to-cell signaling. *NIDA Notes: National Institutes of Health, National Institute of Drug Abuse, 21*(4).

Shire US Inc. (2006). Ensuring Appropriate Stimulant Use for ADHD: A Parent's Guide to Being AWARE [Electronic Version], 5. Retrieved January 16, 2008, from http://www.adderallxr.com/about_adderallxr/about-sideeffects.asp.

Teegarden, S. L., Scott, A. N., Bale, T. L. (May 2009). Early life exposure to a high fat diet promotes long-term changes in dietary preferences and central reward signaling. *Neuroscience, 162*(4), 924–932.

Tikkanen, R., Holi, M., Lindberg, N., & Virkkunen, M. (2007). Tridimensional Personality Questionnaire data on alcoholic violent offenders: specific connections to severe impulsive cluster B personality disorders and violent criminality. *BMC Psychiatry, 7*, 36.

APPENDIX A

A Fable with Principles
for Proactive Parenting

In our clinic, we have a conference room where we hold our meetings with parents and family members of addicted children and teenagers. These meetings are often quite intense. Parents are frequently desperate for ways to reach their self-destructing children by the time they've come to us. To help soothe the parents, we put up placards with wise sayings and quotations about values and principles that we believe are important in parenting, especially when faced with the massive challenges presented by an addicted child.

Although we usually don't address these placards directly, we often catch parents reading them and reflecting on them. During the course of treatment, the family members sometimes bring up one or several of the sayings posted in the meeting room. Those that seem to resonate the most are often drawn from fables and stories meant to impart life lessons.

The response by our clients to these quotations has served to remind me that people learn in different ways, and often lessons imparted in simple stories are those that stick with us. The long and rich tradition of learning though stories includes the parables in the Bible, Greek mythology, Aesop's fables, Native American narratives told around campfires, Mother Goose stories, Grimm's fairy tales, *The Little Prince, Alice's Adventures in Wonderland, Jonathan Livingston Seagull,* and *Who Moved My Cheese?*

I've created the following story for those who enjoy such tales. I've used animals as the characters because this eliminates human stereotyping. This story is meant for parents who are searching for guiding principles and values to teach their children, especially those children who are addicted or prone to addictive behaviors.

The Fable

Two North American wolves fell in love and wanted to start a family. The male was Adam, and the female was Babbitt. Both were large and had beautiful gray and white coats of thick fur. Adam and Babbitt had each lost their parents early in life, but both were adopted by a pack, though they became lone wolves after they matured into adults. Still, neither of them had strong bonds to their packs—so they formed their own.

The problem was that neither had learned the traditional rituals and developmental lessons that come with a pack lifestyle. Still, as a smart and resourceful pair, they found their own territory and dug out a comfortable den for protection. Soon, pups were on the way, which triggered a discussion on how to raise them properly.

"As we start our family and parenting lives together," Adam addressed Babbitt, "how should we go about raising our pups to be solid citizens of the pack? After all, they must eventually take up responsibilities of the group and participate as responsible wolves, because our whole family will need a strong community to survive."

"Yes, I have been feeling a little awkward about dealing with the challenges alone," Babbitt answered, smiling. "Normally we would have the pack elders advise us on the principles of pup raising. I was thinking that because we have found our new hunting ground, let us discover our neighbors by traveling throughout our territory and requesting wisdom from them. Granted, they don't know much about wolf-raising, but we could see what higher principles exist."

Adam looked puzzled. "Do you think they would share and not just run from us?" he asked. "After all, some of them might serve as our dinner one day."

Babbitt wagged her tail and licked him on the face. "Yes, there is a community in which we share life, and there is a relationship of survival," she answered, "but let's see if we can overcome some of those issues with love and support. Our basic instincts are to be of service to the greater good, after all, and we often help each other on a higher level. Remember that time we had that forest fire, and you saved those rabbits? And remember that time when the hunters were killing the deer and you found a hiding place for them?"

Adam was not convinced. "Well, I will see if we can find some of our community who will share, but it will be a lot of work," he said. "At least it will be an adventure, and I am curious about the values and principles of other animals."

The Lion's Story

Almost immediately, the wolves came upon a lion. Their natural sense was to run away, and Adam took up the position of defending an argument for retreat, but instead Babbitt started talking to the lion.

"Mr. Lion, we want to have a discussion with you," she said. "However, if you want to eat us, we will retreat and escape. Would you care to talk to us?"

"I am not hunting now," the lion answered, somewhat startled, "and I would love to converse with someone other than another lion. That seems boring at times. What can I do to help you?"

As Babbitt described their situation as new parents wanting to learn principles for raising their pups, the lion appeared to understand completely. "We have the same issues in raising our cubs," he said, offering the following quotation:

Watch your thoughts
They will become words
Watch your words
They will become actions
Watch your actions
They will become habits
Watch your habits
They will become your character

"The key is choice," the lion added, "which means the choice of everything you see, everything you perceive, and everything you believe. Everything you eat and do becomes your history and legacy in life. It means that you make a choice in how you live and the priorities you create in your daily life and all tasks, ranging from hunting prey to reacting to your mate.

"This mystery of choice comes when we decide not to let life just happen to us, but instead to play an active role in determining our own destinies. So even as young lions, we have the power to pull ourselves out of downward spirals and to decide to live more positive and rewarding lives.

"A lion who I grew up with did not have much parental support and got mixed up with a bad pride of lions, which damaged his reputation. One of his elders, an uncle, came forward and mentored him, helping the young lion make wiser choices so that one day he became the leader of his own pride and was widely respected for keeping peace and order.

"This transformation did not happen overnight. The young wayward lion began to turn his life around slowly with small smarter choices under his uncle's guidance. He began to make choices fit for a leader when it came to hunting, choosing friends, and serving as a good example within the younger lions of the pride.

"With each hour and each day," the wise lion said to Adam and Babbitt, "you will make choices that lead to your place in life. It is not chaos or fate. The choice of how you want to live and who you want to be is yours to make each and every minute.

"This is the mystery of choice. The brain patterns itself according to your choices, so be sure to choose wisely, especially in matters of your mental and physical health. The wiser your choices, the clearer and more peaceful your mind will be when challenges arise. And most important, you will have the lucidity to recognize your purpose and mission in life."

Adam and Babbitt were mesmerized by the lion's deep voice and the lessons he imparted.

After a while, Adam finally broke the silence. "That was deep wisdom and I am grateful," he said to the lion. "My future family and I will share your wisdom for many years to come, and I will be grateful to you for each retelling over the generations to come. Thank you."

Before they walked away in silence and awe, Babbitt reached out and touched noses with the lion to express her gratitude.

The Owl's Story

As Adam and Babbitt trotted on, they wondered if the lion's advice was enough to guide them—but then an owl appeared. Babbitt spoke first.

"Owl," she said, "we are searching for wisdom for living and raising our young to fulfill their destinies. Can you help us?"

The owl hooted and squawked a few times, as if he were trying to find his voice. "Why would you think I would know how to raise wolf pups?" he responded. "As you can see, my life is very different from yours."

"We are not looking for the natural ways of life but the spiritual," Adam answered.

"Well, then," replied the owl, "to that I can speak. The elements that are most important in this forest are relationships and trust. To earn the trust of others, you must be trustworthy and you must trust your own judgment. Young of all species are usually very naïve and afraid of the world. That is one of the reasons they seek out friends who have similar thoughts and fears. They fear intimacy because emotional territory is foreign and intimidating to them. They look for clues before trusting someone—and often they focus on external clues such as appearance.

"But trust should not be based on external appearance. You must first trust your own judgment and then look into the heart of those around you before trusting them. The extent to which you can trust your lover to not flirt with another is related to your own level of self-confidence. The extent to which you can share your deepest fears with someone is related to the level of trust you have with that person. To be able to trust others, you must be confident in your own value and your own trustworthiness."

Adam thanked the owl for the advice, and Babbitt only gave a grunt to acknowledge the owl's information. They walked on and eventually settled for the night in the safety of a shallow cave. They fell asleep after sharing stories from their early years, noting that they'd gone through similar phases. They slept with serene smiles on their faces.

The Bear's Story

Just as the wolves awakened the next morning, they heard some thrashing in the bushes. Before they could run, a bear appeared.

"Don't run," the bear said. "The owl told me that you may want to hear my philosophy about growing up. I am eager to have an audience. Please be comfortable while I share my truths."

The bear was an awesome creature, with paws much bigger than Adam's. The wolves calmed themselves as the friendly bear took a seat with his back against a tree. Adam invited the bear to share his philosophy with them. The bear offered a crooked grin.

"I know bears are thought to be fierce creatures, with bad tempers," he began, "but I do have some thoughts to share with you on raising your young."

Adam and Babbitt relaxed and listened intently as the massive bear offered his thoughts.

"No one can make you feel or think anything—only you have the power to control your feelings and thoughts," the bear explained. "That power is all yours. There is always an instinct, sometimes annoying, to blame another for our feelings. When we give in to it, we say things such as, 'You make me mad,' or 'You are driving me crazy.' No one can make you feel anything. You choose your responses. Happiness and sadness are states of mind. I've seen the poorest creatures smile and laugh. I've also seen the most fortunate beasts claim to be miserable. There is no direct link in the brain that automatically makes you feel a specific emotion. Your emotions are the result of how you choose to perceive and respond to your circumstances."

"Wouldn't you have to have a sense of self-confidence to have that control?" asked Babbitt.

"There are some conditions that would make it hard to understand why you might get upset about being bullied," the bear answered. "Being attacked would trigger feelings of anger and fear. But even in those desperate situations, you still have the power to choose your response. When you let someone dictate your emotions, you give power to them to control your life. If someone is aiming a shotgun at me, I guarantee they will have my attention, and if they are threatening me or someone I care about, I may do whatever they say. But they will not control my thoughts or emotions. We have many options in how we respond to adversity and challenges, so we should never take on the role of victims. We can choose to be masters of our own lives."

With that last comment, the bear stood up lumbered away, without saying farewell.

"I'm hungry," Adam said, "and this is too much to swallow on an empty stomach."

"I'm hungry as well," Babbitt responded, "but let's talk about this some more after we've eaten."

After breakfast, the two wolves sat and talked in depth about the bear encounter.

"If we can teach our pups self-control and confidence, I would be happy," said Adam, "but a bear has an advantage in being one of the largest and most powerful creatures in the animal world."

"Self-confidence isn't always the result of strength or dominance," replied Babbitt. "Regardless of your size, you always have control of what you think. That is the freedom we all have, don't you see? You are getting physical control and mental or spiritual control confused. We can always think what we want. No one else can control that."

"I see what you mean. That is like a right God gave us," said Adam. "With our thoughts we can control how we feel instead of being victimized by those stronger or those meaner than us. It is simple and very powerful."

The Dolphin's Story

The wolf pair stopped to drink by a pool that fed into the ocean. As they lapped at the water, a dolphin poked its head up to greet them.

"Hi there, wolves!" the dolphin said. "I seem to have lost my school of friends. They may have returned to deeper waters for the night. But tomorrow they will find me because we can hear each other through miles of water. In the meantime, I could use some company."

"We are traveling as we prepare to start a family, and we are searching for parenting tips from other creatures of all kinds," Babbitt said in response, feeling sorry for the lonely dolphin. "Can you tell us about your species and their practices for raising young fish?"

"First, I am not a fish. I am dolphin—a warm-blooded mammal like yourself," the dolphin replied. "We refer to our babies as 'calves.' But I would be happy to share some of the very important lessons we impart to them. One of these is that each of life's challenges presents an opportunity to grow.

"Life in the water has plenty of pain, and sometimes you get confronted with the meanest of sharks. It is not unusual to lose part of a fin or all of it, which can be depressing. I've had to hide for days in this pool, just so that I could heal. That is actually why I am here now. It can be lonely because we are a very social species, but I've learned to use these times to assess my life and to build strength physically and mentally so that I will not be so vulnerable to shark attacks. You see, I've taken this challenging time and used it to improve myself, which is something my parents taught me. I will pass this lesson on to my own young one day.

"If we don't see challenges as opportunities, it would be easy to fall prey to self-pity and depression, so I think this is something all creatures would want to teach their young. We all face challenges. Sometimes they are the result of our mistakes and misjudgments, but even then if we can forgive ourselves, learn from the experience, and move ahead feeling stronger, then I believe there is nothing we cannot overcome. I believe our Creator gives us challenges so that we will learn and grow from them, evolving as species and individuals. If our lives were carefree, I don't think we would do that.

"One of the highly probable aspects of life is that things will change. Another is that on some days, we will experience pain and hardship. It may be to humble you, or to teach you something. I would bet on the last assumption. Life is full of blessings, and pain and hardship may be blessings that are difficult to understand at first."

The wolves and dolphin talked well into the night until Adam fell asleep and snored. Babbitt and the dolphin agreed to look for each other again sometime near this spot on the water.

The next morning the dolphin was gone. Adam and Babbitt ended their journey and returned home to apply the lessons imparted from other creatures as they raised their family. They knew that they would make mistakes, as all parents do, but they took to heart all the wise advice given to them, and they dedicated themselves to being as loving and caring parents as possible.

The Fable of the Perfect Child

You can't make a perfect child, because all humans have free will. As parents, you can only hope to instill values in your children that will carry them through the challenges they face. Addiction is one of the greatest challenges to confront individuals and families. You must practice forgiveness of yourself and your child as you work to overcome addiction. Seek all of the advice you can find, but follow your heart and act out of love.

Recently, my family bought a new rabbit, and we find it funny to watch her stand on her hind legs to try to see what is on the other side of the "pillow fence" we use to barricade her running track. Like this bunny, we all want to know what lies on the other side—or in the future. Yet it is impossible to know what life has in store for us, which is both exciting and scary.

I had a heart attack at age 55 and "died" because of the lifestyle I was leading. This terrible experience turned out to be one of the best things that ever happened to me because it forced me to assess my life and to change many of my habits, behaviors, and thought patterns. I hadn't anticipated having the heart attack, nor had I ever expected to think of it as a blessing.

You Can't Change the Past, and You Can't Know the Future

When we are small children, we look to our parents for reinforcement of our behaviors, both good and bad. The feedback we receive in both cases helps determine our character. If our parents teach us that money is the source of happiness, for example, we may be driven to focus on that as adults, even if we are richer than most small nations. There are good reasons why lottery winners often say their lives have not improved, or have even worsened, with wealth. Many of them can't enjoy the money because they feel unworthy of it. In many cases, they squander it.

If our goals are to achieve wealth or power, then we may be looking for external things to give us internal happiness. Our happiness must be generated from within. Millions of dollars won't make you happy if you don't feel worthy of love and happiness. You can rise to be the CEO of the most powerful company on Earth and still feel insignificant and unloved if you are empty inside.

It is also important to know that you are not doomed by your past. Mistakes you made in the past can only affect your future if you allow them to do so. Every day is a new opportunity to *do* better and to *be* better. Drug addiction may have held you or someone you love back in the past, but it does not have to limit your future.

Regardless of how much you work the statistics and calculate probabilities, you can't predict with any accuracy what the future holds. If you are counting on the same things happening in ten years that are happening today, I will bet against you—and I will win. One of the keys to finding happiness for recovering addicts, and for all people, is to enjoy the blessings of the moment without being burdened by either unpleasant memories from the past or expectations for the future.

Be here with the rest of us. What that means to a teenager is to become mindful of experiences in the present: make choices in the present, and don't deny or ignore the needs of today.

✦ ✦ ✦

APPENDIX B

Top 20 Drugs and Their Street Names

(Courtesy of Casa Palmera Treatment Center in Del Mar, California.)

1. Cocaine
Blow, C, candy, coke, do a line, freeze, girl, happy dust, Mama coca, mojo, monster, nose, pimp, shot, smoking gun, snow, sugar, sweet stuff, white powder.

2. Crack (a form of cocaine, smokable)
Base, beat, blast, casper, chalk, devil drug, gravel, hardball, hell, kryptonite, love, moonrocks, rock, scrabble, stones, tornado.

3. Depressants
Backwards, blue heavens, downie, drowsy high, green dragons, idiot pills, joy juice, M&M, no worries, peanut, rainbows, red bullets, stoppers, stumbler, tooles, yellow.

4. Fentanyl
Apache, China girl, Chinatown, dance fever, friend, goodfellas, great bear, he-man, jackpot, king ivory, murder 8, poison, tango and cash, TNT.

5. GHB (Gamma-hydroxybutyric acid)

Caps, cherry meth, ever clear, easy lay, fantasy, G, G-riffic, gamma hydrate, Georgia home boy, grievous bodily harm, liquid ecstasy, liquid X, soap, sodium oxybate.

6. Heroin

Aunt Hazel, big H, black pearl, brown sugar, capital H, charley, china white, dope, good horse, H, hard stuff, hero, heroina, little boy, mud, perfect high, smack, stuff, tar.

7. Inhalants

Air blast, bolt, boppers, bullet bolt, climax, discorama, hardware, heart-on, highball, honey oil, huff, laughing gas, medusa, moon gas, Satan's secret, thrust, whiteout.

8. Ketamine

Bump, cat killer, cat valium, fort dodge, green, honey oil, jet, K, ket, kit kat, psychedelic heroin, purple, special "K," special la coke, super acid, super C, vitamin K.

9. LSD (lysergic acid diethylamide)

A, Acid, black star, blotter, boomers, cubes, Elvis, golden dragon, L, microdot, paper acid, pink robots, superman, twenty-five, yellow sunshine, ying yang.

10. Marijuana

420, Aunt Mary, baby, bobby, boom, chira, chronic, ditch, ganja, grass, greens, hash, herb, Mary Jane, nigra, pot, reefer, rip, root, skunk, stack, torch, weed, zambi.

11. MDMA (methylenedioxy-methamphetamine)

Adam, bean, blue kisses, clarity, club drug, disco biscuits, E, Ecstasy, hug drug, love drug, lover's speed, Mercedes, New Yorkers, peace, roll, white dove, X, XTC.

12. Mescaline

Beans, buttons, cactus, cactus buttons, cactus head, chief, love trip, mesc, mescal, mezc, moon, peyote, topi.

13. Methamphetamine

Beannies, blue devils, chalk, CR, crank, crystal, crystal meth, fast, granulated orange, ice, meth, Mexican crack, pink, rock, speckled birds, speed, tina, yellow powder.

14. Methcathinone

Bathtub speed, Cadillac express, cat, crank, ephedrone, gagers, go-fast, goob, qat, slick superspeed, star, the C, tweeker, wild cat, wonder star.

15. Opium

Ah-pen-yen, aunti, big O, black stuff, Chinese tobacco, chocolate, dopium, dover's deck, dream gun, hard stuff, hocus, joy plant, O, ope, pin yen, toxy, zero.

16. PCP (phencyclidine)

Angel dust, belladonna, black whack, CJ, cliffhanger, crystal joint, Detroit pink, elephant tranquilizer, hog, magic, Peter Pan, sheets, soma, TAC, trank, white horizon, zoom.

17. Psilocybin/psilocin

Boomers, God's flesh, little smoke, magic mushroom, Mexican mushrooms, mushrooms, musk, sherm, shrooms, silly putty, simple simon.

18. Ritalin

Crackers, one and ones, pharming, poor man's heroin, R-ball, ritz and ts, set, skippy, speedball, ts and ritz, ts and rs, vitamin R, west coast.

19. Rohypnol

Circles, forget-me pill, la rocha, lunch money drug, Mexican valium, pingus, R2, Reynolds, roche, roofies, rope, ruffles, wolfies.

20. Steroids

Abolic, anadrol, arnolds, bolasterone, dihydrolone, equipose, gym candy, juice, methyl testosterone, proviron, pumpers, stackers, therobolin, weight trainers, winstrol V.

♦ ♦ ♦

APPENDIX C

Recovery Resources

12-Step Organizations

Al-Anon/Alateen Family Group

www.al-anon.org

888-4AL-ANON

Helps families and friends of alcoholics recover from the effects of living with the problem drinking of a relative or friend. Alateen is a similar program for youth. Call for meeting places and times in the U.S. and Canada.

Alcoholics Anonymous

www.alcoholics-anonymous.org

212-870-3400

A fellowship of men and women who want to stay sober. AA is nonprofessional, self-supporting, nondenominational, multiracial, apolitical, and available virtually everywhere.

Cocaine Anonymous

www.ca.org

310-559-5833

Adapted from the AA program. The only requirement for membership is the desire to stop using cocaine and all other mind-altering substances.

Families Anonymous
www.familiesanonymous.org
800-736-9805
A program for family members and friends concerned about someone's current, suspected, or past drug, alcohol, or related behavioral problems. Call for meetings in the U.S. and Canada.

Nar-Anon Family Groups
www.nar-anon.org
800-477-6291
Designed to help relatives and friends of addicts recover from the effects of living with an addicted relative or friend.

Websites

Above the Influence
www.abovetheinfluence.com
Supports kids in resisting peer pressure to take drugs and drink. Gives detailed information about recreational drugs and their influence.

The Partnership at Drugfree.org
www.drugfree.org
Resource for information on drug-abuse prevention, intervention, treatment, and recovery. Designed to help parents and caregivers effectively address alcohol and drug abuse with their teens and young adults.

National Inhalant Prevention Coalition
www.inhalants.org
Referral and information clearinghouse. Excellent source of information for parents and educators on

what to watch for, including symptoms and dangers of inhalant misuse.

National Institute on Alcohol Abuse and Alcoholism
www.niaaa.nih.gov
Offers publications, research information, and resources.

National Institute on Drug Abuse
www.drugabuse.gov
Supports and conducts research on drug abuse and addiction. Free publications are available, including materials for parents and teachers.

Love First
www.lovefirst.net/wpt
An informative website for families interested in intervention. Includes a bookstore with recommended reading, as well as links to articles, treatment programs, and more.

Treatment Programs

Below is a list of some treatment programs you may want to consult with about your case. Before choosing any treatment option, be sure to review the program, pricing, and staff to determine if it is the best choice for you or your loved one.

Adolescent treatment programs

Caron Adolescent Treatment Center, Wernersville, PA
www.caron.org
800-678-2332

Designed for youth ages 12 to 19; situated in a mountain setting; and offering group, individual, and family therapy. An on-site teaching staff provides alternative classroom instruction and contact with the patients' home school district. Caron is a gender-separate program and offers an extended-care program.

Visions Adolescent Treatment Center, Malibu, CA
www.visionsteen.com
866-889-3665
Serves males and females, ages 12 to 17, with drug and alcohol addiction, behavioral problems, and co-occurring disorders. Intensive structured program situated in a supportive, homelike environment. Also offers a scholastic academy for students needing assistance.

Hazelden Center for Youth and Families, Plymouth, MN
www.hazelden.org
800-257-7810
Residential and outpatient treatment for youth ages 14 to 24. Services include primary care, extended care, and parent education. Also offers a parent program as well as Teen Intervene, designed to provide education, support, and guidance to teens who have experienced mild to moderate chemical use.

Young-adult treatment programs (for ages 18–25)

Origins Recovery Centers, South Padre Island, TX
www.originsrecovery.com
888-U-GET-WELL
Longer-term inpatient, residential, and outpatient treatment programs focused on adult and collegiate-age adults who are struggling with addiction to alcohol and other drugs, including those with dual diagnosis. Origins' multidisciplinary treatment includes medical,

psychiatric, and clinical care; nursing; neuroplasticity-
-based programs; and more. Treatment programs include
a 15-month follow-up and support service.

La Hacienda Treatment Center, Hunt, TX
www.lahacienda.com
800-749-6160

An inpatient program in the Texas Hill Country
offering both adult and collegiate programs. Christian
focus optional. Clinical service includes working with
co-occurring disorders.

Help Lines

Childhelp National Child Abuse Hotline: 800-422-4453

Call if you are a child being abused, a parent about
to lose control, a survivor of abuse feeling suicidal, or an
adult looking for parenting tips.

Substance Abuse and Mental Health Services Administration: 800-729-6686

Information specialists are trained to answer questions about alcohol- and substance-abuse prevention,
intervention, and treatment. They also refer crisis calls
to appropriate sources.

National Council on Alcohol and Drug Dependence: 800-NCA-CALL

24-hour referral to local NCADD affiliates who can
provide information and referrals to services in callers'
areas.

National Runaway Safeline: 800-621-4000

Call if you are a teenager who is thinking of running
away from home, if you have a friend who has run away
and is looking for help, or if you are a runaway ready to

go home. Support and education is also available for parents of teens who have run away or who are threatening to run away.

National Suicide Prevention Lifeline: 800-273-8255

A 24-hour, toll-free suicide prevention service available to anyone in suicidal crisis, as well as to family and friends who are concerned about a loved one who may be experiencing these feelings.

Leading Certification Bodies for Interventionists

Association of Intervention Specialist Certification Board

www.aiscb.org

Offers the Board Registered Interventionist (BRI).

The ARISE® Intervention Model and Certification

www.linkinghumansystems.com/arise

Offers a three-phase process to lead a loved one into appropriate treatment and recovery.

✦ ✦ ✦

ACKNOWLEDGMENTS

As with any project, there are many people to thank, some dating back 40 years when I had my own horrific experiences with an out-of-control teenager. I was humbled by the wisdom of a counselor who knew what she was doing. Since then, I have researched and spent hours learning from other perceptive therapists and teachers as I've developed the programs and techniques presented in this book.

As always, my first thanks goes to my partner in life, Susan, who continues to support me in my healing career. She is a professional as well, and seems to understand my intensity and thoughts without explanation. Susan is a skilled researcher who has helped me find resources and knowledge.

My best friend for all seasons across more than 40 years, Dr. Phil McGraw, has supported me in all my trials, errors, and discoveries.

Barbara Peavey has been my work partner. An amazing clinician, she constantly informs me with her knowledge of human nature and science.

Ben Levenson, CEO of the Origins Recovery Centers, where I served as director of psychology and neurological plasticity programs, is an amazing thinker who is not afraid to believe in miracles. He has allowed me to follow my dreams of developing brain plasticity pro-grams for his center. With his support, we have helped many patients recover and reclaim joy in their lives.

Laura Martinez is a colleague at the Origins Recovery Centers and does tremendous work with the patients. She read the manuscript in its raw form and directed some of the contents. My associate Anthony Haskins, Resource Director at *Dr. Phil,* has provided great editorial support for these projects.

The one who made it all come together was Wes Smith, with whom I have worked over the years. He is the ultimate in wordsmithing.

And to Shannon Marven and Jan Miller, my literary agent team, who have been there for me every time I think of a book, coaching me through the publishing process. Thanks a ton.

❖ ❖ ❖

ABOUT THE AUTHOR

Dr. Frank Lawlis has focused on clinical and research methods exploring the mind-body relationship since 1968, when he received his Ph.D. in psychology with an emphasis in medical psychology and rehabilitation. He is board-certified by the American Board of Professional Psychology in both counseling psychology and clinical psychology. He also received the status of Fellow from the American Psychological Association for his scientific contributions to the field of clinical psychology and behavioral medicine, as well as other awards for his pioneering research in this field.

Dr. Lawlis co-founded the Lawlis Peavey PsychoNeuroPlasticity Center in Lewisville, Texas, and is currently also Director of Psychological and Neurological Plasticity Programs at the Origins Recovery Centers in South Padre Island, Texas. Dr. Lawlis is the principal content and oversight advisor of the *Dr. Phil* show and makes regular appearances on the show.

Dr. Lawlis has authored and co-authored more than 100 articles in peer-reviewed journals and numerous books, including *The ADD Answer* (Viking, 2004), *The IQ Answer* (Viking, 2006), *Mending the Broken Bond* (Viking, 2007), *Retraining the Brain* (Plume, 2009), *The Brain Power Cookbook* (Plume, 2009), *The Autism Answer,* and *PTSD*

Breakthrough (Sourcebooks, 2010). Dr. Lawlis has also created various audio works, available at www.Mind BodySeries.com.

Having served on five prestigious medical-school faculties in the departments of psychiatry, orthopedic surgery, and rehabilitation medicine and five graduate psychology faculties, Dr. Lawlis has blazed new studies and approaches in the care of patients with chronic and acute pain as well as cancer and psychosomatic problems. The medical schools he served include New York University Medical Center (1967–68), Texas Tech University Health Sciences Center School of Medicine (1973–75), University of Texas Health Science Center at San Antonio (1975–76), University of Texas at Dallas (1979–89), and Stanford University School of Medicine (1991–93).

Website: www.franklawlis.com

✦ ✦ ✦

HAY HOUSE TITLES OF RELATED INTEREST

YOU CAN HEAL YOUR LIFE, the movie,
starring Louise L. Hay & Friends
(available as a 1-DVD program and an expanded 2-DVD set)
Watch the trailer at: www.LouiseHayMovie.com

THE SHIFT, the movie,
starring Dr. Wayne W. Dyer
(available as a 1-DVD program and an expanded 2-DVD set)
Watch the trailer at: www.DyerMovie.com

✦ ✦

EMPOWERED YOUTH: A Father and Son's Journey to Conscious Living, by Michael Eisen and Jeffrey Eisen

HEALING YOUR FAMILY HISTORY: 5 Steps to Break Free of Destructive Patterns, by Rebecca Linder Hintze

THE INDIGO CHILDREN TEN YEARS LATER: What's Happening with the Indigo Teenagers!, by Lee Carroll and Jan Tober

THE LAST DROPOUT: Stop the Epidemic!, by Bill Milliken

LIGHT THE FLAME: 365 Days of Prayer, by Andrew Harvey

ONE MIND: How Our Individual Mind Is Part of a Greater Consciousness and Why It Matters, by Larry Dossey, M.D.

THE SECRET LIVES OF TEEN GIRLS: What Your Mother Wouldn't Talk about but Your Daughter Needs to Know, by Evelyn Resh, CMN, MPH, with Beverly West

THE 7 SECRETS OF SOUND HEALING, by Jonathan Goldman
(book-with-CD)

All of the above are available at your local bookstore,
or may be ordered by contacting Hay House (see next page).

✦ ✦

We hope you enjoyed this Hay House book. If you'd like to receive our online catalog featuring additional information on Hay House books and products, or if you'd like to find out more about the Hay Foundation, please contact:

Hay House, Inc., P.O. Box 5100, Carlsbad, CA 92018-5100
(760) 431-7695 or (800) 654-5126
(760) 431-6948 (fax) or (800) 650-5115 (fax)
www.hayhouse.com® • www.hayfoundation.org

✦ ✦

Published and distributed in Australia by: Hay House Australia Pty. Ltd., 18/36 Ralph St., Alexandria NSW 2015 • *Phone:* 612-9669-4299 *Fax:* 612-9669-4144 • www.hayhouse.com.au

Published and distributed in the United Kingdom by: Hay House UK, Ltd., Astley House, 33 Notting Hill Gate, London W11 3JQ • *Phone:* 44-20-3675-2450 • *Fax:* 44-20-3675-2451 www.hayhouse.co.uk

Published and distributed in the Republic of South Africa by: Hay House SA (Pty), Ltd., P.O. Box 990, Witkoppen 2068 *Phone/Fax:* 27-11-467-8904 • www.hayhouse.co.za

Published in India by: Hay House Publishers India, Muskaan Complex, Plot No. 3, B-2, Vasant Kunj, New Delhi 110 070 • *Phone:* 91-11-4176-1620 • *Fax:* 91-11-4176-1630 • www.hayhouse.co.in

Distributed in Canada by: Raincoast Books, 2440 Viking Way, Richmond, B.C. V6V 1N2 • *Phone:* 1-800-663-5714 • *Fax:* 1-800-565-3770 • www.raincoast.com

✦ ✦

<u>Take Your Soul on a Vacation</u>

Visit www.HealYourLife.com® to regroup, recharge, and reconnect with your own magnificence.
Featuring blogs, mind-body-spirit news, and life-changing wisdom from Louise Hay and friends.

Visit www.HealYourLife.com today!